MORE SCOTTISH SETTLERS
1667–1827

by
David Dobson

CLEARFIELD

Printed for
Clearfield Company, Inc. by
Genealogical Publishing Co., Inc.
Baltimore, Maryland
2005

International Standard Book Number: 0-8063-5286-8

Made in the United States of America

INTRODUCTION

Scottish emigration to North America, which began in the early seventeenth century, was small scale and sporadic until the middle of the eighteenth century, after which date it became significant. Scots could be found throughout the continent from Hudson's Bay to Darien, in Panama, as well as throughout the West Indies. This compilation concentrates on settlement in what in due course became the USA and Canada.

Most of the Scottish emigrants seem to have been able to finance their own passages across the Atlantic, but a minority went as indentured servants. Research into Scottish newspapers of the eighteenth century has revealed a number of advertisements for both indentured servants and fare-paying passengers, as shown in the following quotation:

"For Boston, New England, The ship Jean, burthen about 100 tons, 12 men, 4 guns, John McArthur master, now lying in the Harbour of Greenock, is ready to take in goods and will sail for the said place by latter end of August instant. Freighters and passengers may agree with Laurence Dinwiddie jr, merchant in Glasgow, and with Mr James McEwan, bookseller in Edinburgh, or Mr William Robertson at his shop in the Landmarket, Edinburgh. And if any tradesmen or boys have a mind to transport themselves as servants they shall have all due encouragement from the said persons." [*Edinburgh Evening Courant*, #413, of 31 July 1721]

"Ropemakers that are willing to go to Maryland under indentures for 4 to 5 years shall have good wages, bed and board and washing found them during the time of their service...a foreman shall have £25 sterling per annum plus bed, board and washing'" [*The Caledonian Mercury*, #4238]

Sometimes felons were given—and quickly grasped—the opportunity of being released from prison on condition of going abroad as servants. This situation, too, was reported in local newspapers. Notice the following example, taken from *The Caledonian Mercury*, #2929:

"That day [5 January 1739] 13 women and a boy enacted to transport themselves from the House of Correction to the Plantations."

On occasion people with specific skills would be sought:

"Wanted to go the Maryland. A gardener, well recommended and properly qualified, to take care of a gentleman's garden. A married man will be preferred. His passage will be paid and genteel encouragement given. Apply to the publisher."
[*Aberdeen Journal*, #2022 of 9 October 1786]

Only a handful of indentureship agreements have survived in Scotland; most of them presumably went with the indentured servants when they emigrated. One of the few that exist in Scottish archives is the following, which pertains to a man sent to work in Maryland on behalf of a Glasgow-based merchant engaged in the tobacco trade:

"Agreement between Daniel, son of Alexander Campbell of Kilbride and John Glasford, merchant in Glasgow, with the consent of Robert Campbell of Ashnish, binds himself to serve John Glasford as assistant factor or supercargo in Maryland for 4 years from 1 January 1770 with bed and board and £30 wages at termination with liberty to import on his own £20 of goods per annum, with free passage there and back. Subscribed in Glasgow 20 September 1769."
[National Archives of Scotland, NRAS.0396.TD180/20]

Many prospective emigrants were attracted by the opportunity to own land in the New World. Newspapers carried offers such as the following taken from the *Aberdeen Journal* of July 1784:

"Lands for sale in Nova Scotia and the United States. 100 acre lots on the Connecticut River, Vermont, see John Pagan, merchant in Greenock."

The exact number of emigrants from Scotland to the Americas in the seventeenth and eighteenth centuries is not known but is thought to be in the region of 150,000 people.

This book helps to identify some of them. *More Scottish Settlers, 1667–1827* is predominantly based on primary source material located in Scottish archives, especially the records of the Court of Session, Scotland's highest civil court. These records were not used in the compilation of *The Original Scots of Early America, 1612–1785* or the *Scottish Settlers in North America, 1625–1825* series because of major practical difficulties. However, in recent years staff members of the National Archives of Scotland have produced abstracts which have greatly facilitated research into such documents. While the majority of references come from the Court of Session records, there is a minority taken from other sources located within the National Archives of Scotland, in particular Sheriff Court records, Registers of Sasines, Gifts and Deposits, Register of the Great Seal, and Home and Health Department records, as well as burgh records. This book also contains items found in the National Library of Scotland, as well as a few early ship passenger lists held in Canadian archives, supplemented by material taken from contemporary newspapers.

David Dobson,
St Andrews, Scotland, 2005.

REFERENCES

AyrBR = Ayr Burgess Roll

AJ = Aberdeen Journal, series

AUL = Aberdeen University Library

BD = Book of Dunvegan, [Aberdeen, 1909]

BM = Blackwood's Magazine, series

BPP = British Parliamentary Papers, series

DPCA= Dundee, Perth & Cupar Advertiser, series

DGA = Dumfries & Galloway Archives

EA = Edinburgh Advertiser, series

ECA = Edinburgh City Archives

EEC = Edinburgh Evening Courant, series

ERA = Edinburgh Register of Apprentices

EUL = Edinburgh University Library

EWJ = Edinburgh Weekly Journal, series

F = Fasti Ecclesiae Scoticanae, [Edinburgh, 1915]

GA = Glasgow Archives

GCr = Glasgow Courier, series

GJ = Glasgow Journal, series

GM = Glasgow Mercury, series

IC   =   Inverness Courier, series

IJ   =   Inverness Journal, series

JCTP=   Journal of the Commissioners for Trade and the Plantations, series, [London]

KCA =   King's College, Aberdeen

LPL =   Liverpool Public Library

MdGaz   Maryland Gazette, series

MUG =   Munimenta Alme Universitatis Glasguensis, Vol.3, [Glasgow, 1854]

NAS =   National Archives of Scotland, Edinburgh

NLS =   National Library of Scotland, Edinburgh

PAC =   Public Archives of Canada

PANB=   Public Archives of New Brunswick

PC   =   Perth Courier, series

PCC =   Prerogative Court of Canterbury, London

RGG =   Roll of Graduates of Glasgow University, 1727-1897, [Glasgow, 1898]

RGS=   Register of the Great Seal of Scotland

S   =   Scotsman, series

SHR =   Scottish Historical Review, series

SM   =   Scots Magazine, series

SP   =   The Scots Peerage, [London, 1904]

SPAWI   Calendar of State Papers, America & the West Indies, series

For PICTOU HARBOUR in Nova Scotia, BOSTON and FALMOUTH in New England.

THE Ship HECTOR, John Speir master, burthen 200 tons, now lying in the harbour of Greenock. For freight or paſſage apply to John Pagan merchant in Glaſgow, Lee, Tucker, and Co. merchants in Greenock; and in order to accommodate all paſſengers that may offer, the ſhip will wait until the 10th of May next, but will poſitively ſail betwixt and the 15th of that month.

N. B. Pictou harbour lyes directly oppoſite to the iſland of St. John's, at the diſtance of 15 miles only.

MORE SCOTTISH SETTLERS
1667-1827

ABELL, WILLIAM, in Prince George's County, Maryland, an indentured servant of Richard Henderson factor for John Glassford at Bladensburg, Maryland, 1766. [NAS.GD237/21/51/15]

ABERCROMBIE, ALEXANDER, surgeon's mate in Nova Scotia, 1749. [JCTP#57/112]

ABRAMS, WILLIAM, in Miramachi, New Brunswick, 1821. [NAS.SC53.56.3/cx]

ADAM, ROBERT, born in Scotland 1739, a gentleman and an early settler of Alexandria, Virginia, died on 27 February 1789. [PIG#1016]

ADAMS, WILLIAM, a cooper late in New York now in Halifax, Nova Scotia, 1786. [NAS.CS17.1.5/303]

ADAMSON, JOHN, in Caldwell County, USA, 1818. [NLS.Acc.7595]

ADAMSON, JOHN, a surgeon in Slateford now in America, 1820. [NAS.CS17.1.39/414]

ADDISON, ROBERT, a goldsmith in Virginia, 1778. [NAS.CS16.1.173/327]

ADDISON, Reverend, arrived in New York from Greenock on the <u>George</u>, Captain Boag, 12 July 1774. [SM.36.446]

ADIE, ALEXANDER, from Dunfermline, Fife, then in

America 1796. [NAS.CS17.1.15/267]

AGNEW, MARY, a prisoner in Dumfries Jail, guilty of child-murder, to be transported to Virginia in 1745. [DGA.Jailbook GF4/21]

AINSLIE, THOMAS, from Edinburgh, the Customs Collector of Quebec, probate 1 December 1806, Prob.11/1452 PCC

AIRD, HUGH, son of Robert Aird of Crossflat, died in Montreal 9 July 1820. [EEC#17039][S.4.188]

AITCHISON, ANDREW, from Glasgow, then in Boston, 1800. [NAS.CS17.1.18/412]

AITCHISON, THOMAS, a merchant in Virginia, 1782. [NAS.CS17.1.1/97]

AITCHISON, WILLIAM, in Norfolk, Virginia, 1807. [NAS.CS17.1.26/377]

AITKEN, GEORGE, third son of George Aitken portioner of Bridgend of Dalkeith, Midlothian, now in Fayette, Kentucky, 1820. [NAS.CS17.1.39/222]

AITKEN, JAMES, merchant in New York, 1789. [NAS.CS17.1.8/346]

AITKEN, JOHN, a weaver in Dalkeith then in America, 1820. [NAS.CS17.1.39/222]

AITKEN, MATTHEW, in America, 1783, son of James Aitken in Sandholes. [NAS.CS17.1.2.30]

ALEXANDER, HECTOR, in Dumfries, Prince William County, Virginia, brother of John Alexander of Mountpleasant then in Greenock, 1824. [NAS.RS54.1985]

ALEXANDER, JOHN, in New York, 1726. [NAS.RH9.1.221]

ALEXANDER, WILLIAM, in Richmond, Virginia, 16 February 1786. [NAS.GD58.1.16]

ALEXANDER, WILLIAM, late in St Lucia, and by 1790 on the River Dorsie, America. [NAS.CS17.1.9,368]

ALLAN, JAMES, sr., a cabinetmaker in Fredericksburg, Virginia, 1787. [NAS,CS17.1.6,268]

ALLAN, JAMES, cabinetmaker in Fredericksburg, Virginia, 1788. [NAS.CS17.1.7/308]

ALLAN, THOMAS, a merchant in Norfolk, Virginia, 1803. [GA.T-ARD#13/1]

ALLAN, Mrs THOMAS, late of Tweeddale, Peeblesshire, died in Hoboken, New York, September 1822. [EEC#17482]

ALLAN, WILLIAM, a weaver from Glasgow, settled in Dalhousie township, Upper Canada, around 1821. [BPP.2.167]

ALLISON, JOHN, born in Perth, a merchant, died in Montreal 20 February 1817. [S.1.16][AJ#3617]

ALSTON, WILLIAM, son of James Alston of Muirburn, died in New York 24 November 1820. [S.4.203]

ANDERSON, ALEXANDER, a farmer, settled in East Florida 1767. [NAS.NRAS.771, bundle 402]

ANDERSON, ALEXANDER, a forger, banished to the Plantations for life, at Aberdeen, February 1768. [AJ#1051]

ANDERSON, ANDREW, a merchant in Virginia, 13 July 1765. [NAS.RD4.198.558]

ANDERSON, GEORGE, indentured as a servant for 6 years in Virginia, in the Canongate, Edinburgh, 1 August 1745. [NAS.B59.29.82]

ANDERSON, HUGH, of Bridgecastle, Linlithgow, heir to late Dr Anderson in St Kitts, was appointed as Inspector of the Public Gardens and Mulberry Plantations in Georgia, 1736. [EEC#1988]

ANDERSON, JAMES, in New York, 1726. [NAS.RH9.1.221]

ANDERSON, JAMES, a merchant from Leith, then in America, 1795. [NAS.CS17.1.14,140]

ANDERSON, JAMES, Hudson Bay, 23 July 1796. [NAS.RS.Orkney#385]

ANDERSON, JAMES, jr., a merchant from Forres, died in Augusta, North America, 19 July 1823. [DPCA#1104]

ANDERSON, JOHN, a planter in Antigua, appointed Mr John Anderson, writer in Glasgow, as his factor, subs. in Antigua 29 April 1714, witnesses, Robert Arthur, Robert Alexander, and Andrew Geills. [NAS.RD2.104.724]

ANDERSON, JOHN, from Dumfries to Virginia on the Nanie and Jenny, master William Maxwell, 23 May 1749. [NAS.CS96/2161/9]

ANDERSON, JOHN, a merchant in Leith, brother of James Anderson, and a merchant in Virginia 1791. [NAS.RS.Caithness#211]

ANDERSON, ROBERT, a housebreaker imprisoned in Edinburgh Tolbooth, indented with Thomas Gardiner, a merchant in Edinburgh, for service in Virginia, 1744. [NAS.HH.11/22]

ANDERSON, SARAH, daughter of Robert Anderson in Kent County, Maryland, 1819. [NAS.CS17.1.38/547]

ANDERSON, WILLIAM, sheriff in New York 1708. [Bodleian MS. Clarendon#102/164]

ANDERSON, WILLIAM, settled in Ramsay township, Upper Canada, by 1825. [BPP.2.167]

ANDERSON, Mrs, possibly from Dundee, drowned in the wreck of the brig Margaret, near Sable Island 29 October 1821. [AJ#3841]

ANGUS, AGNES, spouse of James Finlay now in America, daughter of Robert Angus a merchant in Kirkintilloch, 1788. [NAS.CS17.1.7,187]

ANGUS, ANDREW, settled in Lanark township, Upper Canada, around 1820. [BPP.2.164]

ANNESLEY, WALTER, thief in Banff, banished to the Plantations for life, at Aberdeen May 1766. [AJ#959]

ARMOUR, JAMES, in Perth Amboy, 23 July 1707. [NAS.RS.Argyll.92.381]

ARMSTRONG, LAURENCE, Lieutenant Governor of Nova Scotia, probate 28 November 1741, Prob.11/713 PCC

ARTHUR, JAMES, eldest son of Robert Arthur a victualler in Glasgow, settled in North America by 1803. [NAS.CS17.1.22/78]

AUCHMUTY, JAMES SMITH, a gentleman in Shelburne, Nova Scotia, probate 15 December 1790, Prob.11/1198 PCC

AULD, WILLIAM, at Hudson Bay, 3 November 1802. [NAS.RD4.272.723]

BAILLIE, GEORGE, born 1775, with his family of nine, from Sutherland, emigrated from Cromarty on the <u>Ossian of Leith,</u> master John Hill, from Cromarty to Pictou in June 1821. [IJ:29.6.1821]

BAILLIE, ISABEL, daughter of Thomas Baillie in Ferrytown of Cree, wife of Samuel McLean a merchant in Wigton then in America, 1782. [NAS.CS17.1.1.367]

BAILLIE, JAMES, son of Robert Baillie a merchant in Edinburgh, a merchant in Jamaica from 1740 to the 1750s, then a planter on Bagbie Plantation on the Newport River, Georgia. [NAS.GD1.1155.64-68]

BAILLIE, Mrs MARGARET, born 1766, a widow with her family of nine, from Sutherland, emigrated from Cromarty on the <u>Ossian of Leith</u>, master John Hill, to Pictou in June 1821. [IJ:29.6.1821]

BAILLIE, ROBERT, son of George Baillie of Hardington, a merchant in Jamaica from 1751 to 1753, then a planter on Bagbie Plantation on the Newport River, St Andrews parish, Georgia, later a Lieutenant of the Georgia Rangers 1758. [NAS.GD1.1155/65-71]

BAILLIE, WILLIAM, a gypsy and a housebreaker who escaped from Dumfries Tolbooth, later imprisoned in Edinburgh Tolbooth, taken for shipment to the East or West Indies by warrant of baillie Dundas, 16 May 1715. [ETR/NAS.HH11]

BAIN, ALEXANDER, a merchant in Virginia, 11 November 1774. [NAS.RS.Dunbarton.11.109]; also in 1798, [NAS.CS17.1.17/190]

BAIN, GEORGE, born 1790, a laborer in Greenock, emigrated from Port Glasgow to St John, New Brunswick, on the Favorite of St John, master John Hyndman, 22 October 1815. [PANB:MS.RS23E/f9798]

BAINSLIE, BETTY, a thief, wife of Robert Patterson a fuller, imprisoned in Haddington Tolbooth then in Edinburgh Tolbooth, released for transportation via Glasgow to the Plantations 3 September 1773. [ETR/NAS.HH11.29]

BAIRD, ARCHIBALD, a planter in South Carolina, probate 11 March 1788, Prob.11/1163 PCC

BAIRD, JAMES, a merchant in Virginia, eldest son of John Baird. 1782, 1788. [NAS.CS17.1.1/97; CS17.1.17,159]

BAIRD, JAMES, of Broompark, formerly in Virginia, died 1817. [S.1.21]

BAIRD, PATRICK, late of Philadelphia, admitted as a burgess of St Andrews 2 October 1759. [StABR]

BAIRD, RICHARD FREDERICK, youngest son of Sir James Gardner Baird of Saughtonhall, died in Bermuda 15 June 1819. [AJ#3731]

BAIRD, WILLIAM, of Greencroft, Petersburg, Virginia, second son of John Baird late merchant on the James River, Virginia, grant of Easter Muckcroft on 4 July 1807. [RGS.138.4.4]

BAKER, JAMES, a merchant in Philadelphia, 1822. [NAS.SC48.49.25.17/77]

BALLANTYNE, JOHN, a merchant in Westmoreland, Virginia, 1789/1790. [NAS.CS17.1.8,221; CS17.1.9/48]

BANKS, ALEXANDER, in America 1807. [NAS.CS17.1.26/381]

BARCLAY, Reverend JOHN, son of Reverend Dr Barclay in Kettle, Fife, died in Kingston, Upper Canada, 26 September 1826. [AJ#4116]

BARCLAY, NINIAN, on Sir William Alexander's expedition to Nova Scotia 1627. {see court case re John Buchanan, a merchant, who had supplied Alexander's men with clothes and other necessities and had accepted salt in part payment} [Dunbarton Burgh Records, 7 January 1628]

BARR, DAVID, born 1791, a laborer in Port Glasgow, emigrated from Port Glasgow to St John, New Brunswick, on the Favorite of St John, master John Hyndman, 22 October 1815. [PANB:MS.RS23E/f9798]

BARR, JOHN, in Bridge of Weir, to emigrate via Quebec to Upper Canada, 1820. [NAS.SC58.75.79]

BARR, ROBERT, in Bridge of Weir, to emigrate via Quebec to Upper Canada, 1820. [NAS.SC58.75.79]

BARR, WILLIAM, in Petersburg, Virginia, 1806. [NAS.CS17.1.25/352]

BAVERLEY, WILLIAM, in Virginia, admitted as a burgess and guilds-brother of Glasgow on 12 September 1781. [GBR]

BEATON, ANGUS, tenant of Lord MacDonald in Clachan, Skye, bound for America around 1802. [NAS.GD221.4433.1]

BEATON, NIEL, from South Uist, emigrated from Tobermory on the Emperor Alexander of Aberdeen, master Alexander Watt, to Sydney, Cape Breton, in July 1823, arrived there on 16 September 1823. [IJ:30.1.1824]

BEATTY, WILLIAM, a former apprentice to Irving Logan in Dumfries, absconded to Virginia, alleged father of Margaret Stobrick's child, 29 July 1737. [NAS.CH2.537.2.84]

BELL, JAMES, tenant in Nether Whitton, then in America 1799. [NAS.CS17.1.18/325]

BENT, LUKE, born 1800 in Montreal, arrived at Greenock on 21 August 1821, a student of physic in Edinburgh. [ECA.SL115.2.2/98]

BENZIE, JOHN, born in Aberdeen 1791, a merchant in Halifax, Nova Scotia, died at sea on the Diadem, Captain Wallace, 28 October 1827. [AJ#4165]

BETHUNE, Reverend JOHN, minister at Williamstown, Charlottenburg County, Glengarry, Upper Canada, probate 15 March 1816, Prob.11/1578 PCC

BIGGAR, ROBERT, a tanner from Dumfries, now in America 1790. [NAS.CS17.1.9/48]

BIRSS, JAMES, born in Kincardineshire, a merchant, died in Montreal 22 January 1821. [AJ#3818]

BISSET, JOHN, a young Scot, admitted as an Episcopalian clergyman in Newport, Rhode Island, 20 March 1786. [AJ#2024]

BLACK, DAVID, a merchant in Boston, 1783. [NAS.CS17.1.2.233]

BLACK, JAMES, in Sinclairtown, Fife, then in USA 15 July 1819. [NAS.RS.Kirkcaldy#2/109]

BLACK, JOHN, merchant in St John, New Brunswick, co-owner of the Lord Macartney of Greenock, the William of Greenock, & the Cato of Greenock, 1798, and of the Liberty of Greenock 1800. [NAS.CE60.11.5/64/71/187; 6/17]

BLACK, JOHN, in Halifax, Nova Scotia, co-owner of the Sophy of Greenock, 1804, the Lady Parker of

Greenock, 1804, the Caledonian of Greenock, 1804, the Lilly of Greenock 1804, and the Thomas of Greenock, 1805. [NAS.CE60.11.8/58/64/5/9/10]

BLACK, JOHN, a merchant in South Carolina, 1823. [NAS.CS17.1.43/10]

BLACK, JOHN NEWBURY, in America, 1826. [NAS.RD5]

BLACK, WILLIAM, from Dumfries, later in America, 1794. [NAS.CS17.1.13,233]

BLACKIE, WILLIAM, born 1792, late a merchant in Glasgow, died in New York 31 May 1823. [EEC#17474][DPCA#1092]

BLACKWOOD, JOHN, late of Quebec, Member of the Council of Lower Canada, died in Bath on 25 June 1819. [S.3.128]

BLACKWOOD, JOHN, son of John Blackwood of Airdsgreen, Lanarkshire, emigrated from Rothesay to Quebec on the Fair Canadian in June 1780. [NAS.NRAS#0067/1]

BLAIR, ALEXANDER, born 1783, died in Quebec 30 May 1810. [Dundonald, Ayrshire, g/s]

BLAIR, ARCHIBALD, in Richmond, Virginia, 1796, 1802, eldest son of James Blair deceased, grandson of Archibald Blair a writer in Edinburgh deceased. [NAS.CS17.1.15/273; CS17.1.21/270]

BLAIR, BUCHANAN, born during 1793, a laborer in Doune, Stirlingshire, emigrated from Port Glasgow to St John, New Brunswick, aboard the Favorite of St John, master John Hyndman, on 22 October 1815. [PANB:MS.RS23E/f9798]

BLAIR, ELIZABETH, daughter of Patrick Blair in Boston,

1750. [NAS.RD3.210.373]

BLAIR, JOHN, thief in Banff, banished to the Plantations for life, at Aberdeen May 1766. [AJ#959]

BLAIR, MONCRIEFF, of the Montreal Bank, son of Reverend John Blair in Colmonell, died during October 1821. [S.5.258]

BLAIR, PATRICK, a doctor in Boston, father of Elizabeth 1 February 1750. [NAS.RD3.210.373]

BLANE, THOMAS, a merchant in New York, then in London, 1787. [NAS.CS17.1.6/271]

BOARDMAN, JOHN, mate of the privateer Active of New York, testament confirmed on 24 October 1780 with Commissariat of Glasgow

BOGUE, JOHN, a carpenter at Bogue's Tower, Alexandria, Virginia, son of Robert Bogue portioner of Auchencraw, son of Benjamin Bogue portioner of Auchencraw, 1805. [NAS.CS17.1.24/447]

BOUCHIER, ALEXANDER, a merchant in Newfoundland, 1802, grandson of Alexander Bouchier a shipmaster in Crawfordyke. [NAS.RS81.23]

BOWIE, GEORGE, sometime a merchant in Kilmarnock, Ayrshire, now in America, June 1787. [NAS.CS17.1.6,153]

BOWIE, WILLIAM, late baillie of the Gorbals, now in Halifax, Nova Scotia, 1785/1787. [NAS.CS17.1.4/195; CS17.1.6]

BOWIS, ROBERT, a surgeon in Virginia, son of Robert Bowis, minister of Rattray 1699-1741, and Margaret Campbell. [F.4.171]

BOWMAN, DAVID, naval officer and HM Customs Surveyor at Port Accomack, Virginia, subscribed to a deed of factory in favour of James Balfour in Kirkcaldy, Fife, on 15 April 1771. [NAS.B41.7.8/159]

BOWMAN, JAMES OSWALD, in Georgetown, Montgomery County, Maryland, appointed Miss Isabella Bowman of Kirkcaldy, Fife, as his attorney on 10 May 1796. [NAS.B41.7.9]

BOWMAN, JOHN, jr., son of Provost Bowman of Glasgow, settled in East Florida 1769. [NAS.NRAS.771, bundle#295]

BOWMAN, JOHN, son of John Bowman of Ashgrove, Ayrshire, died in Charleston, South Carolina, 1807. [AJ#3120]

BOY, ALEXANDER, a tenant farmer, a prisoner in Inverness during 1709, transported to America. ["Old Ross-shire and Scotland" p.97, W. McGill,, Inverness, 1909]

BOYD, ADAM, nephew of William Boyd in Townhead of Symington, in America by 1797. [NAS.CS16.1.16/132, 177]

BOYD, SPENCER, eldest son of James Boyd, physician at West Point, York River, Virginia, 1778, [NAS.CS16.1.173/148]; of Penkill, now in King and Queen County, Virginia, 1789. [NAS.CS17.1.8/172]

BOYLE, ANDREW, the dempster and executioner of Stirling, a thief, banished to the Plantations for life, at Stirling in May 1768. [AJ#1060]

BRACCO, JOHN, at St Michael's River, Maryland, 1767. [NAS.NRAS.0021]

BRAND, JOSEPH, son of John Brand in Virginia, educated

at Marischal College, Aberdeen, during 1793.
[MCA.372]

BREBNER, JOHN, from Leith, then a merchant in Halifax,
1786. [NAS.CS17.1.5/224]

BROADFOOT, WILLIAM, a merchant in Norfolk, Virginia,
great grandson of John Broadfoot, a merchant in
Wigton, 1799. [NAS.RS.Wigton#544]

BRODIE, HUGH, in Montreal 1814. [NAS.SC58.4.218]

BRODIE, JOHN, born 1782 in Granville County, North
Caarolina, arrived in Liverpool on 26 December 1802,
resident of 6 James Square, Edinburgh, by 17 March
1803. [ECA:SL115.2.1/141]

BRODIE, JOHN, from Knockmairshill, Greenock, settled in
America by 1810. [NAS.CS17.1.29/326]; possibly
settled in Montreal by 1814. [NAS.SC58.4.218]

BROW, THOMAS, a merchant in King and Queen County,
Virginia, now in Fenwick, Ayrshire, 1783.
[NAS.CS17.1.2.145]

BROWN, Mrs CATHERINE, born during 1797, wife of
Lawrence George Brown, died in Beauharnois,
Montreal, on 10 February 1827. [AJ#4134]

BROWN, CLAUDE SCOTT, born during 1795, Assistant
Commissary General, died in Kingston, Upper
Canada, on 7 July 1821. [S.5.244]

BROWN, DAVID, in St Johns, New Brunswick, inventory 18
November 1813 Edinburgh [NAS.SC70.1.9.92]

BROWN, Dr GUSTAVUS, in Maryland on 9 December
1756. [NAS.RD4.197.404]

BROWN, JAMES, jr., a merchant in Augusta, Georgia,

1789, son of James Brown sr., deceased, merchant there, probably from Paisley. [NAS.SC58.58.3/4]

BROWN, Dr **JAMES MURRAY**, died in Virginia on 23 April 1824. [Fife Herald#120]

BROWN, **JOHN**, a merchant in Virginia, 1783. [NAS.CS17.1.2.83]

BROWN, **JOHN**, of Netherwood, Dumfries-shire, died in Richmond, Virginia, on 25 December 1822. [DPCA#1072]

BROWN, **MARGARET**, in Maryland, on 9 August 1763. [NAS,RD4.4.198.246]

BROWN, **THOMAS**, late in Virginia, now in Fenwick, Ayrshire, 1782. [NAS.CS171.11.395]

BROWN, **THOMAS**, in King and Anson counties, Virginia, ca1790. [NAS.NRAS.0623.T-MJ.304]

BROWN, **WILLIAM**, a merchant in Virginia, 1783. [NAS.CS17.1.2.83]

BROWN, or **GRAHAM**, Mrs, a sorner imprisoned in Edinburgh Tolbooth, released on condition of leaving Scotland 5 March 1742. [NAS.HH11/21]

BROWNLEE, **JAMES,** eldest son of Reverend James Brownlee in Falkirk, Stirlingshire, matriculated at Glasgow University in 1817, graduated MA in 1822, emigrated to USA as a probationer of the Secession Church, later a minister in Staten Island, New York. [MAGU#296]

BRUCE, Dr **CHARLES KEY**, late of Calcutta, died on Staten Island, New York, on 21 December 1826. [AJ#4131]

BRUCE, JOHN, merchant in Norfolk, Virginia, during 1787, 1789. [NAS, CS17.1.6, 357; CS17.1.8/29]

BRUCE, NORMAND, in Frederick County, America, 1796. [NAS.CS17.1.15/137]

BRUCE, ROBERT, shoemaker, thief, sentenced in Edinburgh to 7 years transportation in September 1739, [CM#3034]

BRUCE, Mrs SELKRIG, born in 1751, relict of Robert Dock of Prora, East Lothian, died in New Windsor, Maryland, on 24 April 1825. [EEC#17748]

BRYCE, ARCHIBALD, in Richmond, Virginia, 17... [NAS.B10.12.4.fo.124/127]

BRYDIE, ALEXANDER, a merchant in America, 1796. [NAS.CS17.1.15/216]

BRYDIE, WILLIAM NAPIER, late of Richmond, Virginia, 1822. [NAS.CS17.1.42/319]

BUCHAN, JOHN, dyster in Oib, to America on the Diamond of Glasgow, master Robert Arthur, in 1740. [NAS.SC54.48.14]

BUCHANAN, ALEXANDER, in New York then in Campbeltown, Argyllshire, testament confirmed 27 January 1819. [NAS.CC2.3.14.224]

BUCHANAN, ARCHIBALD, of Drumhead, formerly a merchant in Williamsburg and in Norfolk, Virginia, on 27 September 1751. [NAS.RS10.Dunbarton.8.250]

BUCHANAN, DONALD, tenant of Lord MacDonald in Peenorcronan, Skye, bound for America around 1802. [NAS.GD221.4433.1]

BUCHANAN, DONALD, born during 1794, a laborer in

Kenmore, Perthshire, emigrated from Port Glasgow to St John, New Brunswick, aboard the Favorite of St John, master John Hyndman, on 22 October 1815. [PANB:MS.RS23E/f9798]

BUCHANAN, Dr GEORGE, of Auchintorlie, a physician in Maryland afterwards in Hilton, 17 May 1739. [NAS.RS10.Dunbarton.7.325]

BUCHANAN, GEORGE, a tanner from Glasgow, then in Petersburg, Virginia, 1792, 1809. [NAS.CS17.1.12,177; CS17.1.29/76]

BUCHANAN, JAMES, a merchant in Falmouth, Virginia, 11 November 1758. [NAS.RS10.Dunbarton.9.160]

BUCHANAN, JAMES, a planter in Jamaica, by 1801 in Virginia. [NAS.CS17.1.9/14]

BUCHANAN, JAMES, born during 1791, a laborer in Kenmore, Perthshire, emigrated from Port Glasgow to St John, New Brunswick, on the Favorite of St John, master John Hyndman 22 October 1815. [PANB:MS.RS23E/f9798]

BUCHANAN, Reverend JOHN, in Manchester, Virginia, 1812. [NAS.CS17.1.31/273]

BUCHANAN, MARION, a prisoner in Edinburgh Tolbooth, indented with William Ged for service in the Plantations on 27 February 1745. [NAS.HH11/22]

BUCHANAN, MARY, in New York, 1820, [NAS.CS17.1.39/324]; 17 May 1827. [NAS.RD5.341.296]

BUCHANAN, NEIL, died in Petersburg, Virginia, 23 February 1793. [GJ#2765]

BUCHANAN, ROBERT, a merchant from Glasgow, then in

Halifax, 1786. [NAS.CS17.1.5/45]

BUCHANAN, ROBERT, from Glasgow, now in Maryland, 1790. [NAS.CS17.1.9/150]

BUCHANAN, ROBERT, born during 1794, in Balquhidder, Perthshire, emigrated from Port Glasgow to St John, New Brunswick, on the Favorite of St John, master John Hyndman, on 22 October 1815. [PANB:MS.RS23E/f9798]

BUCHANAN, WILLIAM, of Auchinmar, sometime a merchant in Glasgow, then in North America, 1785. [NAS.CS17.1.4/125]

BUCHANAN, WILLIAM, a merchant in Glasgow, in Virginia by 1790. [NAS.CS17.1.9,115]

BUCHANAN, WILLIAM, in Maryland, 1794. [NAS.CS17.1.13,294]

BUCHANAN, WILLIAM, possibly from Paisley, Renfrewshire, a saddler in Petersburg, Virginia, 1809. [NAS.CS17.1.29/76]

BUNZEA, WILLIAM, a weaver and portioner of Newstead, later in the Jignor Valley, Westmore County, Pennsylvania, by 1799. [NAS.CS17.1.18/377]

BURD, JAMES, sometime Colonel of a Provincial Regiment in Pennsylvania, 19 June 1766. [NAS.RS27.173.177]

BURFORD, W.R., in Canada, 30 June 1828. [NAS.RD5.421.205]

BURGESS, WILLIAM, born during 1791, a laborer in Port Glasgow, emigrated from Port Glasgow to St John, New Brunswick, on the Favorite of St John, master John Hyndman, 22 October 1815. [PANB:MS.RS23E/f9798]

BURGESS, ..., born 1794, a laborer in Port Glasgow, emigrated from Port Glasgow to St John, New Brunswick, on the Favorite of St John, master John Hyndman, 22 October 1815. [PANB:MS.RS23E/f9798]

BURN, FINLAY, Captain of the New York Volunteers, 1786. [NAS.CS17.1.5/23]

BURNETT, JOHN, born during 1800, an engineer, son of Thomas Burnett a civil engineer in Montreal, died at the Rideau Canal, Upper Canada, 9 December 1827. [AJ#4180]

BURNETT, Dr WILLIAM, in West Florida, 1772. [NAS.RS.Dumfries.xxi.285, etc]

BURNSIDE, ALEXANDER, a merchant in Quebec, 1813. [NAS.CS46/1862.8.29]

BURR, ROBERT, born during 1796, arrived in St John, New Brunswick, in November 1815 on the Favorite of St John, master John Hindman, from Scotland. [PANB:MS.RS555/c4]

BURT, ANDREW, in Baltimore, eldest son of the late John Burt, tacksman of Pittencrieff Colliery, 1811. [NAS.CS17.1.31/57]

BURT, JOHN, in North America 1805, son of Henry Burt. [NAS.CS17.1.24/457]

CAIRD, JAMES, a merchant in Alexandria, Virginia, 1800. [NAS.CS17.1.18/219]

CAIRD, JAMES, a writer from Stranraer, married Christian, second daughter of Archibald McNeil, in California on 9 October 1810. [SM.72.877]

CAIRD, JOHN, a baker in Alexandria, Virginia, 1800.

[NAS.CS17.1.18/219]

CAIRNS, WILLIAM, of Torr in the Stewartry of
Kirkcudbright, a merchant in New York, 1820.
[NAS,CS17.1.39/203]

CALDERCLEUGH, ANDREW, in Pennsylvania, 1789.
[NAS.CS17.1.8/182]

CALDERCLEUGH, ROBERT, in Pennsylvania, 1789.
[NAS.CS17.1.8/182]

CALDWELL, JOHN, emigrated to New England before
1723. [NAS.CH1/2/62/41]

CAMERON, DONALD, emigrated on the brig Alexander of
Greenock in June 1772, landed at Charlottetown,
Prince Edward Island, 25 June 1772.
[PAPEI#2664/140]

CAMERON, DOUGLAS, emigrated on the brig Alexander of
Greenock in June 1772, landed at Charlottetown,
Prince Edward Island, 25 June 1772.
[PAPEI#2664/140, 152]

CAMERON, JOHN, born around 1735, an indentured
servant who absconded from John Lamond, Anne
Arundel County, Maryland, in January 1755.
[MdGaz#509]

CAMERON, JOHN, born 1782, a laborer in Kenmore, wife
Margaret born 1788, children Robert born 1805, Mary
born 1807, Jean born 1809, Peter born 1811,
emigrated from Port Glasgow to St John, New
Brunswick on the Favorite of St John, master John
Hyndman, 22 October 1815.[PANB:MS.RS23E/f9798]

CAMERON, ROBERT, from Edinburgh, then in America
1796. [NAS.CS17.1.15/267]

19

CAMPBELL, ALEXANDER, in Prince George County, Maryland, 18 July 1757. [NAS.RD3.224.480]

CAMPBELL, ALEXANDER, late a merchant in Virginia, thereafter in Glasgow, testament confirmed in 1785 with the Commissariat of Glasgow. [NAS]

CAMPBELL, ALEXANDER, from Islay, later in America, father of Polly, Catherine and Jean, 1796. [NAS.CS17.1.15/182]

CAMPBELL, ALEXANDER, born 1794, Kincairn, Perthshire, emigrated from Port Glasgow to St John, New Brunswick, on the Favorite of St John, master John Hyndman, 22 October 1815. [PANB:MS.RS23E/f9798]

CAMPBELL, ALEXANDER, arrived in St John, New Brunswick, in November 1815 on the ship Favorite of St John, master John Hindman from Scotland. [PANB.MS.RS555/c4]

CAMPBELL, ANDREW, late in Baltimore, 1794. [NAS.CS17.1.13,140]

CAMPBELL, ARCHIBALD, in New York, 1726. [NAS.RH9.1.221]

CAMPBELL, ARCHIBALD, merchant in Bermuda, 1784. [NAS.CS17.1.3/375]

CAMPBELL, ARCHIBALD, merchant in Baltimore, Maryland, 1789. [NAS.CS17.1.8/335]

CAMPBELL, ARCHIBALD, a merchant in Virginia. 1819. [NAS.CS17.1.38/458]

CAMPBELL, ARCHIBALD, merchant in New York, 1820. [NAS.CS17.1.39/213]

CAMPBELL, CHRISTINA, spouse to Alexander McCalman, late in Lochausay now in America, 1793. [NAS.CS17.1.12,337]

CAMPBELL, COLIN, son of John Campbell a colonist in Jamaica, a student at Glasgow University during 1720. [MUGU#219]

CAMPBELL, COLIN, jr., formerly a merchant in Glasgow, then in Virginia 1790. [NAS.CS17.1.9,60]

CAMPBELL, COLIN, in St John, New Brunswick, 1795. [NAS.GD1.512.28]

CAMPBELL, DAVID, a bookseller in Boston, New England, and a benefactor of Glasgow University during 1692. [MUG#442]

CAMPBELL, DAVID, Writer to the Signet, in America 1786, 1790. [NAS.CS17.1.5/23; CS17.1.9/41]

CAMPBELL, DONALD, son of Malcolm Campbell in Fortingall, Perthshire, servant to ... McDonald, a Jacobite - captured at Preston in 1715, transported to the West Indies, settled in New England, died there before 1748. [Caledonian Mercury, January 1748]

CAMPBELL, DONALD, son of Archibald Campbell, in Norfolk, Virginia, 1789. [NLS.5036.fo67/70]

CAMPBELL, DUNCAN, in New York 1700. [Rawlinson MS/A272/108]

CAMPBELL, DUNCAN, Argyll, settled in New York 1775. [NAS.NRAS.0934, bundle 509/580]

CAMPBELL, DUNCAN, from Moerlanich, Breadalbane, Perthshire, emigrated to America in 1807. [NAS.GD119/11/8/2/17-18]

CAMPBELL, FINLAY, in Ballechroisk, Breadalbane, Perthshire, to 'emigrate to America' in 1802. [NAS.GD112/11/7/5/15]

CAMPBELL, FREDERICK, in Kirnan, Westmoreland County, Virginia, 19 January 1819. [NAS.RS.Argyll#2995]

CAMPBELL, ISABELLA, wife of George Logan in Norfolk, Virginia, 1792. [NAS.CS17.1.12,109]

CAMPBELL, JAMES, of Burnbank, a prisoner in Edinburgh Tolbooth, to be transported to the Plantations, 1725. [ECA.Moses#158/6045-6047]

CAMPBELL, JAMES, a merchant in Virginia and debtor of the late James Douglas a merchant in Glasgow 1769. [see James Douglas's testament confirmed 21 April 1769 in Glasgow]

CAMPBELL, JAMES, born 1791, a laborer in Killin, Perthshire, with wife Mary born 1787, and children James born 1809, Alexander born 1811, and James born 1813, emigrated from Port Glasgow to St John, New Brunswick, on the Favorite of St John, master John Hyndman, 22 October 1815. [PANB:MS.RS23E/f9798]

CAMPBELL, JOHN, a merchant from Glasgow then in America, 1783. [NAS.CS17.1.2.236]

CAMPBELL, Colonel JOHN, of Glendaruel, Argyll, late of the 42nd Regiment, Superintendent of Indian Affairs in Lower Canada, died in Montreal on 23 June 1795. [CM#11541; 22.8.1795] [EEC:22.8.1795]

CAMPBELL, JOHN, Auchinwillen, died near Three Rivers, Canada, on 17 October 1819. [S#3/151][EA#5845]

CAMPBELL, JOHN, a merchant from Glasgow, later in

Montreal, 1823. [NAS.CS17.1.43/12]

CAMPBELL, JOHN, in Pictou, Nova Scotia, married Marion, second daughter of Malcolm Campbell of Cornaig, Coll, on 31 January 1826. [EEC#17860]

CAMPBELL, LAURENCE, from Glasgow, died in Charleston during 1804. [AJ#2647]

CAMPBELL, MUNGO, died in Kinloch, Nova Scotia, in 1810. [EEC]

CAMPBELL, POLLY, eldest daughter of Alexander Campbell from Islay, Argyllshire, settled in America, married ..... Murnford, by 1800. [NAS.CS17.1.19/263]

CAMPBELL, ROBERT, a stationer, died in Philadelphia on 14 August 1800. [EEC]

CAMPBELL, ROBERT, in Richmond, North America, third son of Dr Robert Campbell of Smiddy Green, 1801. [NAS.CS17.1.20/310]

CAMPBELL, WALTER, born 1745, late Captain of the Prince of Wales American Regiment of Foot, died in Perth on 18 May 1823, husband of Nancy de Veber [1774-1828]. [Greyfriars gravestone, Perth]

CAMPBELL, WILLIAM, son of John Campbell a colonist in Jamaica, a student at Glasgow University during 1724. [MUGU#227]

CAMPBELL, WILLIAM, a merchant in St Johns, New Brunswick, 1813. [NAS.SC58.26.165]

CANT, JAMES, a wright in Edinburgh, banished to HM Plantations in America for life, released from Edinburgh Tolbooth for transportation there by Peter Colquhoun, on 25 June 1773. [ETR/NAS.HH11/28]

CARLYLE, ALEXANDER, a merchant and a planter in Virginia, father of Adam Carlyle of Lymekills, heir to his granduncle William Carlyle, a merchant and a planter in Virginia or Maryland, 27 May 1767. [NAS.S/H]

CARMICHAEL, JOHN, born 1729, escaped from St Mary's County Jail, Maryland, in December 1749. [MdGaz#242]

CARMICHAEL, ROBERT, a merchant in Virginia, 18 August 1770. [NAS.RS10.Dunbarton.10.295]

CARMICHAEL, WALTER, late of America, now at Grange, Edinburgh, 16 April 1765. [NAS.RD2.198.1117]

CARRUTHERS, JAMES, a merchant in Savannah, 1819. [NAS.CS17.1.39/552]

CAW, ALEXANDER, late merchant in Leith, died in Charleston, South Carolina, on 18 August 1817. [S.1.42]

CHALMERS, ALEXANDER WHITE, died in Lesmahagow, only child of David Chalmers, formerly of Dundee now of Richmond, Virginia, testament confirmed on 18 December 1820. [NAS.CC14.5.20.277]

CHALMERS, DAVID, from Auchtermuchty, Fife, a printer in New York 1822-. [NAS.NRAS.0462.10]

CHALMERS, Mrs JOHN, a widow, formerly of Broomfield, Glasgow, died in Philadelphia on 13 August 1819. [EA#5833]

CHAPMAN, Dr NATHANIEL, Philadelphia, was admitted as a burgess and guildsbrother of Ayr on 4 October 1802. [ABR]

CHARLES, DUNCAN, in Alexandria, Virginia, around 1802, eldest son of Duncan Charles a baker in Musselburgh,

Midlothian. [NAS.CS17.1.21/268]; in 1808 in
Alexandria. [NAS.CS17.1.27/252]

CHARLES, GEORGE, late in Alexandria, Fairfax County,
Virginia, then a butcher in Musselburgh, Midlothian, by
1797. [NAS.CS17.1.16/213]

CHEYNE, Miss, born during 1749, eldest daughter of
Charles Cheyne a merchant in Edinburgh, grand-niece
of Dr George Cheyne, died in Lunenburg, Nova
Scotia, on 8 January 1821. [S.5.226]

CHISHOLM, JAMES, emigrated from Loch Broom to
America in 1775, arrived in Philadelphia on 6 October
1775, a Revolutionary Army officer, in New York 1789.
[NAS.NRAS.771, bundle 700]

CHISHOLM, WILLIAM, a merchant in Virginia later in
Pittenweem, Fife, 1794. [NAS.CS17.1.13/450]

CHRISTIE, ADAM, jr., a merchant in Pensacola, 1778.
[NAS.CS16.1.173/159]

CHRISTIE, WILLIAM, MA, born during 1760 in Aberdeen, a
journalist, died in Montreal on 5 May 1829. [AJ#4251]

CLARK, JOHN, born during 1739, a merchant in Halifax,
Nova Scotia, died in Roxburgh near Boston, New
England, on 19 May 1761. [AJ#710]

CLARK, THOMAS, a merchant in New England, 1695.
[NAS.GD3.4.469]

CLEGHORN, JOHN, Frederick County, Maryland, probate
25 May 1824, Prob.11/1685, PCC

CLOUSTOUN, THOMAS, a skipper in Newberry, New
England, son of Robert Cloustoun a carpenter and
sailor in Stromness, Orkney, 1787.
[NAS.RS.Orkney#133]

COATS, GEORGE, late in St Johns, now in Glasgow, 1823. [NAS.CS17.1.42/15]

COCHRANE, DAVID, a merchant in Virginia, heir to Henry Cochrane of Barbachlaw, 1784, 1789/1790. [NAS.CS17.1.3/314; CS17.1.8,359; CS17.1.9,82]

COCHRANE, ELIZABETH, daughter of John Cochrane of Kirktonfield, married William Morris, Perth, Upper Canada, at Kirktonfield 15.8.1823. [DPCA#1099]

COCHRANE, JAMES, son of ... Cochrane and Isabel Gairn in Errol, Perthshire, a steward on HMS Betsey, died in Savannah, Georgia, probate January 1781 PCC

COCHRANE, JOHN, a physician in St Bartholemew's, Colleton County, South Carolina, probate 8 September 1762, Prob.11/879

COCHRANE, RICHARD, late of New Jersey, now in Glasgow, 1782. [NAS.CS17.1.1/91]; 1793, [NAS.CS17.1.12,412]

COCHRANE, RICHARD, an American Loyalist, former judge of the Court of Common Pleas in New Jersey, died in Dalkeith during October 1804. [AJ#2962]

COCHRANE, WILLIAM, in Baltimore 1800. [NAS.CS17.1.18/308]

CODMAN, JOHN, born 1782 in Boston, America, a gentleman, arrived in Liverpool on 28 August 1805, residing at 3 Fyfe Street, Edinburgh, on 30 November 1805. [ECA.SL115.2.2/49]

COLQUHOUN, ALEXANDER, a bleacher at Clochny Field, Dunbartonshire, died at Cornwall, Canada, 26.8.1823. [DPCA#1111]

COLQUHOUN, CECILIA, wife of James Kirkwood a grocer from Glasgow, then in America, 1806. [NAS.CS17.1.25/475]

COLQUHOUN, WALTER, a merchant in Virginia then in Jamaica, 1783. [NAS.CS17.1.2.188]

COLVILLE, CHARLES, born in Arbroath, a seaman on the Dolphin of Philadelphia, Captain O'Bryan, was captured and imprisoned in Algiers during July 1785. In July 1790 he was released from captivity having been ransomed and in September 1790 he arrived at Greenock on the Peggy, Captain Marquis, from Leghorn. [AJ#2230]

CONNEL, WILLIAM, born 1780, a laborer in Port Glasgow, emigrated from Port Glasgow on the Favorite of St John, master John Hyndman, 22 October 1815. [PANB:MS.RS23E/f9798]

CONNER, CHARLOTTE FELICITY, daughter of Captain William Conner, Craney Island, Norfolk County, Virginia, wife of Hugh Sproule Crauford of Cowdenhill, 12 April 1773. [NAS.RS.Dunbarton.10.463]

CONQUEROR, GEORGE, of Mosshall, a surgeon in Maryland 1743. [NAS.RS.Edin.#128/79; 130/210]

CONSTABLE, ALEXANDER, Lieutenant of the Fencible American Regiment, 28 August 1776; 1796 [NAS.RS27.228.161; S17.1.15/113]

COOK, JOHN, in Floshend, Gretna, Dumfries-shire, a rapist, transported to America in 1774. [DGA.GF4.23.23]

COOPER, ALEXANDER, in Georgetown, Maryland, 1796. [NAS.CS17.1.15/385]

COOPER, THOMAS, born around 1730, a sailor,

absconded from the ship Mary, master Thomas Davison, at Lower Marlborough on the Paxutent, Maryland, on 20 May 1749. [MdGaz#213]

CORBET, JOSEPH, a merchant in Virginia, 1782. [NAS.CS17.1.1/97]

CORBETT, ROBERT, a shoemaker in Hamilton, Lanark County, North America, 1800. [GA.T-ARD#13/1]

CORMACK, ENEAS, in Montreal, tenant of Samuel Forbes tacksman of Bankhead of Wick, cnf 15 January 1814. [NAS.CC4.5.1.298]

COUPAR, JAMES, possibly from Leith, then in America, 1794. [NAS.CS17.1.13,44/261]

COUTTS, HERCULES, from Montrose, a merchant in London, died in Newcastle, Pennsylvania, probate 7 October 1709, Prob.11/512 PCC

COVENTRY, or JOHNSTONE, ANN, a thief imprisoned in Edinburgh Tolbooth, indented with Thomas Gardiner, a merchant in Edinburgh, for service in the American Plantations, 1743. [NAS.HH11/22]

COVENTRY, ROBERT, a merchant in Virginia, 1806, 1808. [NAS.CS17.1.25/440; CS17.1.27/104]

COWAN, JOHN, a baker in Falkirk, married Margaret, daughter of James Leishman a carrier and portioner in Falkirk, in 1781, but abandoned her and went to America in 1786. [Process of Declarator of Marriage and Adherence, 1800, Commissariat of Edinburgh, #1182]

COWIE, JANET, in Canada, 6 October 1829. [NAS.RD5.386.513]

COWIE, R., at Hudson Bay, 1828. [NAS.RD5.354/214, 221]

COWIE, W., at Hudson Bay, 1828. [NAS.RD5.354/214, 221]

CRAIG, JAMES, Philadelphia, now a Chelsea pensioner in Sutherland, 1786. [NAS.CS17.1.5/237]

CRAIG, Sir JAMES HENRY, Colonel of the 78th Regiment, Governor of Upper and Lower Canada, probate 20 March 1812, Prob.11/1531 PCC

CRAIG, ROBERT, a merchant in Manchester, Virginia, 1800, son of Robert Craig of Giffin, Beith. [NAS.CS17.1.18/397; CS18.715.2]

CRAIGIE, GEORGE, Orkney, later in Portsmouth, New Hampshire, died before 1834. [NAS.NRAS.0627, box 5, bundle 7]

CRAIGIE, JOHN, died in Quebec, 26 November 1813. [AJ#3450]

CRAM, PATRICK, born 1732, an indentured servant who absconded from the 14th Regiment in Maryland in June 1757. [MdGaz#633]

CRAMOND, JOHN, a merchant in Norfolk, Virginia, 1778. [NAS.CS16.1.173/159]

CRAWFORD, ANDREW, late merchant in St Johns, Newfoundland, son of John Crawford a merchant in Port Glasgow, May 1816. [NAS.SC53.56.1/82]

CRAWFORD, BELLAMY, only son of Daniel Crawford a merchant in South Carolina, matriculated at Glasgow University on 13 November 1756. [MAGU#54]

CRAWFORD, GEORGE, born 1790, arrived in St John, New Brunswick, 11.1815, on the Favorite of St John, master John Hindman, from Scotland. [PANB.MS.RS555/c4]

CRAWFORD, GEORGE, of Climpy, now in North America, 1822. [NAS.CS17.1.42/66]

CRAWFORD, JAMIE, to New England during 1736. [NAS.GD237/20/12/1-7]

CRAWFORD, JOHN, a merchant in Quebec, co-owner of the Two Friends of Greenock, 1800. [NAS.CE60.11.6/99]; a merchant, died in Quebec 1803. [AJ#2921]

CRAWFORD, JOHN, a merchant in Port Glasgow, Newfoundland and Lisbon, sederunt book 1816-1820. [NAS.CS96.335-40]

CRAWFORD, Captain MOSES, a feuar from Irvine, Ayrshire, now in Virginia, 1797. [NAS.CS17.1.16/131]

CREIGHTON, JOHN, in Lunenburg, Nova Scotia, probate 4 July 1808, Probate 11/1482 PCC

CREIGHTON, LUCY, a widow in Lunenburg, Nova Scotia, probate 6 July 1824, prob.11/1688 PCC

CRIGHTON, ALEXANDER, in St Augustine, Florida, 1817. [NAS.CS17.1.36/386]

CROCKETT, CHARLES, intended spouse of Anna Muilman, son of James Crockett in Charleston, South Carolina, 1752. [NAS.RS27.156.466]

CROCKETT, JAMES, from Charleston, a merchant in London, 1754. [NAS.RS27.144.179]

CROCKETT, JOHN, a merchant in Charleston, probate 28 June 1740, Prob.11/703 PCC

CROSS, JAMES, a merchant in Virginia 1800. [NAS.CS17.1.19/113]

CROSS, **Mrs**, died in St John's, Newfoundland, 7 November 1821. [EEC#17241]

CRUDEN, **Reverend ALEXANDER**, sometime Rector of South Farnham, Virginia, late in Aberdeen, testament confirmed on 8 August 1793 with the Commissariat of Aberdeen. [NAS]

CRUICKSHANK, **JAMES**, a chaplain bound for the Leeward Islands 28 February 1694. [CTB#X.1.514]

CUMMING, **ELIZABETH**, wife of Andrew McFarlane of Blairnairn, sometime a merchant in New York, 3 September 1755. [NAS.RS.Dunbarton.3.501]

CUMMING, **JOHN**, from Boisdale, South Uist, from Boisdale, South Uist, emigrated on the brig Alexander of Greenock in June 1772, landed at Charlottetown, Prince Edward Island, 25 June 1772. [PAPEI#2664/151]

CUMMING, **ROBERT**, from Aberdeenshire, settled in Concord, New England, by 1725; a merchant in Boston, New England, father of John who was baptised in March 1728, witnesses Dr John Gordon, John Cumming a merchant, and James Cumming of Barns. [St Paul's Episcopal Church Register, Aberdeen] [NAS.GD105.339]

CUMMINGS, ..., wife and family, arrived in New York on 18 July 1774 from Greenock on the George, Captain Boag. [SM.36.446]

CUNNINGHAM, **ANN**, daughter of John Cunningham, wife of John Johnston a surgeon in Kentucky, 1811. [NAS.CS17.1.31/495]

CUNNINGHAM, **ARCHIBALD**, late of Glasgow, died in New York 13 September 1799. [AJ#2704]

CUNNINGHAM, JOHN, born 1781, from Virginia, died at the home of his grandmother Lady Cunningham of Robertland, 1806. [AJ#3045]

CUNNINGHAM, JOHN, a brewer from Greenock who settled in America by 1786. [NAS.CS17.1.5/193]

CUNNINGHAM, SUSANNAH, daughter of Nathaniel Cunningham in Massachusetts, 1785. [NAS.CS17.1.4/123]

CUNNINGHAM, WILLIAM, son of William Cunningham, land labourer in Stewarton, guilty of burglary, banished to the American Plantations for 7 years, at Ayr on 7 May 1766. [AJ#957]

CUNNINGHAM, WILLIAM, New York, 1789. [NAS.CS17.1.8/49]

CUNNINGHAME, DAVID, second son of Sir John Cunningham of Robertland, emigrated to Virginia or Maryland around 1729, sought in 1751, information to Robert Peter, a merchant in Bladenburg, or William Cunningham, merchant at the Falls of the Rappahannock River. [MdGaz#339]

CURRIE, ARCHIBALD, from Argyll, a merchant in New York, died in Martinique 1802. [EA#4048]

CURRIE, JOHN, from South Uist, emigrated from Tobermory on the Emperor Alexander of Aberdeen, master Alexander Watt, to Sydney, Cape Breton, in July 1823, arrived there on 16 September 1823. [IJ:30.1.1824]

CUSTIS, Colonel JOHN, a merchant in Virginia, 1680. [NAS.RD3.48.513]

CUTHBERT, JOSEPH, in Savannah, Georgia, grandnephew of Alexander Cuthbert of Castlehill, Inverness, 1786. [NAS.RS.Inverness#143]

CUTHBERT, WILLIAM, a merchant in Virginia, 1784. [NAS.CS18.714.23]

CUTHBERTSON, Reverend JOHN, born 1720 in Carnwath, Lanarkshire, ordained at Braehead in 1747, emigrated to America in 1752, died 10 March 1791. [RPC#79]

CUTHBERTSON, WILLIAM, supercargo of the Elizabeth and Katherine, died in Virginia by July 1678. [NAS.RH9.8.229]

DALGLEISH, Mr ALEXANDER, minister at Darien, testament confirmed 1707 in Edinburgh. [NAS]

DALRYMPLE, MARTHA, a widow in Brunswick, North Carolina, probate 12 December 1787, Prob.11/1160

DALZIEL, JOHN, formerly in Frederick's County, Maryland, 1765. [NAS.RS23.XIX.339]

DAVIDSON, ALEXANDER, a mariner in America, son of John Davidson, deceased, a manufacturer in Arbroath, Angus, 1789. [NAS.CS17.1.8/379]

DAVIDSON, PETER, a salt cadger in Strathmiglo, Fife, imprisoned in Edinburgh Tolbooth for the theft of two pieces of linen-cloth, released for transportation from Leith to Maryland 20 Sepember 1769 on the Mally of Glasgow, Captain Peacock. [ETR/NAS.HH11.28]

DAVIDSON, THOMAS, in Pictou, Nova Scotia, 27 November 1807. [NAS.RD2.303.318]

DAVIDSON, THOMAS, born 1791, arrived in St John, New Brunswick, in November1815, on the Favorite of St John, master John Hindman, from Scotland. [PANB.RS555.c4]

DAVIDSON, WILLIAM, a jail breaker, transported to America in 1775. [DGA.GF4.23.35]

DAVIDSON, WILLIAM, released from Edinburgh Tolbooth for shipment to America via Glasgow 24 January 1775. [ETR/NAS.HH11/28]

DAVIE, JAMES, in Bovina, America, 26 June 1828. [NAS.RD5.372.752]

DAVIE, WILLIAM, settled in Dalbeth, Ramsay township, Upper Canada, by 1821. [BPP.2.165]

DAVISON, WILLIAM, Peeblesshire, a Captain of the 52nd Regiment of Foot, died in Boston, pro. July 1776 PCC

DEANS, JOHN, a shoemaker in Orange, New Jersey, 1820. [NAS.CS17.1.39/382]

DEMPSTER, DAVID, late in Gettysburg, America, then in Wester Tillochie, Kinross, 1800. [NAS.CS17.1.19/308]

DENHAM, WILHELMINA, wife of Francis Hall a civil engineer in Queenstown, and daughter of Thomas Denham of the Register Office, Edinburgh, died in Queenstown, Upper Canada, on 31 January1826. [EEC#17865]

DENNY, ALEXANDER, a mariner in Charleston, probate 4 August 1730, Prob.11/639 PCC

DEWAR, COLIN, born 1792, a laborer in Kenmore, Perthshire, emigrated from Port Glasgow to St John, New Brunswick, on the Favorite of St John, master John Hyndman, 22 October 1815. [PANB:MS.RS23E/f9798]

DEWAR, JOHN, born 1786, a laborer in Killin, Perthshire, emigrated from Port Glasgow to St John, New

Brunswick, on the Favorite of St John, master John Hyndman, 22 October 1815. [PANB:MS.RS23E/f9798]

DEWAR, PETER, born 1759, a farmer in Kenmore, Perthshire, with his wife BETSY, born 1765, and children , JEAN, born 1795, a servant in Kenmore, JEAN, born 1792, a servant in Kenmore, JOHN, born 1794, a laborer in Kenmore, MARGARET, born 1796, a servant in Kenmore, JANET, born 1795, a servant in Kenmore, HUGH, born 1799, a laborer in Kenmore, JAMES, born 1785, a laborer in Kenmore, emigrated from Port Glasgow to St John, New Brunswick, on the Favorite of St John, master John Hyndman 22 October 1815. [PANB:MS.RS23E.f9798]

DIACK, ALEXANDER, in Norfolk, Virginia, 1783. [LPL.ms25/271/PA16]

DICK, RICHARD, a carpenter, son of George Dick a shoemaker in Jedburgh, Roxburghshire, then in America 1807. [NAS.CS17.1.26/355]

DICKIE, THOMAS, Halifax, Nova Scotia, 1787, possibly from Greenock. [NAS.RS81/13]

DICKSON, JOHN, Writer to the Signet, died in Kingston, Upper Canada, 8 July 1823. [DPCA#1110]

DICKSON, ROBERT, a fur trader in Upper Canada around 1813. [NAS.NRAS#0069]

DICKSON, THOMAS, late servant to Mrs Drummond in Meadowhope, imprisoned in Linlithgow, guilty of rape, later in Edinburgh Tolbooth, released to go abroad on 4 August 1744. [NAS.HH11/22]

DICKSON, THOMAS, died in Queenstown, Upper Canada, 22 January 1825. [AJ#4038][EEC#17704]; relict Archange Grant in Dumfries testament confirmed on 28 April 1829 with the Commissariat of Dumfries.

[NAS]

DICKSON, WILLIAM, late in Virginia then in Glasgow, was appointed as supercargo of the brig Commerce, Captain McCall, in 1776. [NLS.Acc8793/47]

DOBBIE, JAMES, a weaver from Glasgow, and his family, settled in Lanark, Upper Canada, by 1826. [BPP.2.166]

DOBIE, RICHARD, born 1727, a merchant in Montreal, died 23 March 1805. [AJ#3004]

DOCHARD, DONALD, tenant of Lord MacDonald in Maligar, Skye, bound for America around 1802. [NAS.GD221.4433.1]

DODD, JAMES, son of William Dodd and Margaret Dodd in Berwick-on-Tweed, master of the Nancy and of the Holbeach, in Boston, Massachusetts, probate March 1774 PCC

DOLLAR, WILLIAM, born 1797, a shoemaker in Greenock, emigrated from Port Glasgow to St John, New Brunswick, on the Favorite of St John, master John Hyndman, 22 October 1815. [PANB:MS.RS23E/f9798]

DON, RICHARD, released from Edinburgh Tolbooth for shipment to America via Glasgow 24 January 1775. [ETR/NAS.HH11/28]

DONALD, ALEXANDER, a merchant from Glasgow, then in Richmond, Virginia, 1787. [NAS.CS17.1.6/96, 201; 7/18]

DONALD, ANDREW, in Bedford County, Virginia, 1799, son of William Donald jr., a merchant in Greenock. [NAS.RS81.19]

DONALD, GEILS, daughter of the late Andrew Donald in

Virginia, married George Noble in Greenock 18
September 1821. [EEC#17217]

DONALD, JAMES, a merchant in St Augustine, Florida,
trading to the Mississippi, 31 October 1776.
[NAS.NRAS.0159.C4]

DONALD, ROBERT, a merchant in Virginia, 3 August 1757.
[NAS.RS10.Dunbarton.9.97]; 1789.
[NAS.CS17.1.8/35]

DONALD, ROBERT, a merchant in Pensacola, then in Ayr,
testament confirmed on 10 February 1791 with the
Commissariat of Glasgow. [NAS]

DONALDSON, DUNCAN, born 1794, a laborer in Killin,
Perthshire, emigrated from Port Glasgow to St John,
New Brunswick, on the Favorite of St John, master
John Hyndman, 22 October 1815.
[PANB.MS.RS.23E/f9798]

DONALDSON, JAMES, in Annapolis, Maryland, dead by
1748, father of James. [NAS.RH18.3.236]

DONALDSON, WILLIAM, a merchant in New York, 1758,
later a woollen draper in London. [NAS.CS96/1834,
41]

DONALDSON, WILLIAM, late in St Johns, New Brunswick,
died in Jamaica 18 December 1819. [S.4.167]

DOUGLAS, ANDREW, a merchant in Surinam, inventory 21
January 1706. [NY Wills, Liber 3/4, fo.453/455]

DOUGLAS, ARCHIBALD, son of James Douglas a
merchant in Virginia, granted the lands of Rosehall on
3 February 1795. [NAS.RGS.128/132]

DOUGLAS, DONALD, born 1791, with his family of one,
from Sutherland, emigrated from Cromarty on the

Ossian of Leith, master John Hill, to Pictou, Nova Scotia, in June 1821. [IJ:29.6.1821]

DOUGLAS, GEORGE, a merchant in New York 1782. [NAS.GD185.29.5]

DOUGLAS, JAMES, brother of the Duchess of Douglas, died in Dumfries, Prince William County, Virginia, 18 November 1766. [SM.39.55]

DOUGLAS, JAMES, a merchant in Virginia, 1785, dead by 1788, husband of Katherine, father of Margaret and Katherine. [NAS.CS17.1.4/264; CS17.1.7/20]

DOUGLAS, JAMES, a merchant in New York 1782. [NAS.GD185.29.5]

DOUGLAS, JAMES, from Kirkcudbright, educated at Theological Hall from 1808 to 1812, licensed 1813, a minister at Chirnside, Roxburghshire, emigrated to America in 1818. [RPC]

DOUGLAS, JANET, widow of Kenneth McKenzie of Kilcoy, now wife of James Daley, late in London now in North America, 1789. [NAS.CS17.1.8/285]

DOUGLAS, JOHN, at Fort Stanwix, America, 1759. [NAS.NRAS.0114]

DOUGLAS, JOHN, Customs Controller of Prince Edward Island, 1800. [NAS.CS17.1.19/168]

DOUGLAS, JOHN, in Charleston, South Carolina, husband of Catherine Douglas testament confirmed on 6 September 1816 with the Commissariat of Brechin. [NAS]

DOUGLAS, Mrs MARGARET, in New York, 13 March 1829. [NAS.RD5.384.752]

DOUGLAS, NORMAN, born 1803, with his family of one, from Sutherland, emigrated from Cromarty on the Ossian of Leith, master John Hill, to Pictou, Nova Scotia, in June 1821. [IJ:29.6.1821]

DOUGLAS, SAMUEL, a merchant in New York 1782. [NAS.GD185.29.5]

DOUGLAS, WILLIAM, in Charleston, 27 June 1808. [NAS.RD2.303.634]

DOUGLAS, WILLIAM, in Camden, America, 1809. [NAS.CS17.1.29/138]

DOW, JAMES, an excise officer guilty of fraud, imprisoned in Stirling Tolbooth and later in Edinburgh Tolbooth, released for shipment to America 3 September 1772. [ETR/NAS.HH11/28]

DOW, PETER, an excise officer guilty of fraud, imprisoned in Stirling Tolbooth and later in Edinburgh Tolbooth, released for shipment to America 3 September 1772. [ETR/NAS.HH11/28]

DOW, ROBERT, born 26 May 1753, son of Reverend Robert Dow {1707-1787} and Janet Adie, a physician in New Orleans. [F.3.79]

DOW, STEWART, born 9 November 1748, son of Reverend Robert Dow {1707-1787} and Janet Adie, a merchant in Bermuda, died 18 July 1786. [F.3.79]

DOWNEY, ALEXANDER, in Culpepper County, Virginia, 1806. [GA.T-ARD#13/1]

DREMEN, JOHN, a cotton spinner from Glasgow, then in America, 1800. [NAS.CS17.1.19/208]

DRUMMOND, JAMES, in Virginia, a bachelor, probate February 1667 PCC

DUFF, ALEXANDER, born 1774, son of Reverend Mr Duff the minister of Foveran, a merchant, died in Amherstburg, Upper Canada, on 10 June 1809. [PC#22]

DUFF, CHARLES, in St Mary's, York, New Brunswick, 1826. [NAS.SC48.49.25.22/78]

DUGUID, WILLIAM, in Baltimore then in Aberdeen, testament confirmed on 7 February 1822. [NAS.CC10.7.3.183]

DUNBAR, JOHN, in Albany, 1726. [NAS.RH9.1.221]

DUNBAR, ROBERT, merchant in Virginia, 1789. [NAS.CS17.1.8/198]

DUNBAR, ROBERT, a merchant in Falmouth, Virginia, 1823. [NAS.CS17.1.42/34]

DUNCAN, ALEXANDER, in Fredericksburg, Virginia, 1806. [GA.T-ARD#13/1]

DUNCAN, Dr ANDREW, Edinburgh, admitted as a Fellow of the American Philosophical Society of Philadelphia in 1786. [NAS.GD103/2/450]

DUNCAN, JOHN, a brush manufacturer from Glasgow, then in Maryland 1778. [NAS.CS16.1.173/88]

DUNCAN, THOMAS, a bookseller from Glasgow, then in North America, 1778. [NAS.CS16.1.173/88]

DUNCAN, WILLIAM, a bookseller from Glasgow, then in America, 1783. [NAS.CS17.1.2.289]

DUNCAN, WILLIAM, formerly a merchant in Glasgow, later in Shepherdstown, Maryland, 1790. [NAS.CS17.1.9/68]

DUNCAN, WILLIAM, Spotsylvania, Virginia, probate 23 December 1828, Prob.11/1748 PCC

DUNCANSON, MATILDA, daughter of John Duncanson a physician in Inveraray, died in Washington, America, on 2 August 1799. [AJ#2700][EA#3732]

DUNCANSON, ROBERT, born 1787, a laborer in Callendar, emigrated from Port Glasgow to St John, New Brunswick, on the Favorite of St John, master John Hyndman, 22 October 1815. [PANB:MS.RS23E/f9798]

DUNCANSON, WILLIAM, from Alloa, Clackmannanshire, a thief in Stirling, imprisoned in Edinburgh Tolbooth, indented as a servant with Thomas Gardner, a merchant in Edinburgh, for service in America, 18 March 1742. [NAS.GD112/17/1/11-12/3] [NAS.HH.11/21]

DUNDAS, JAMES, born around 1725, an indentured servant who absconded from William Brogden, in Queen Anne, Maryland, in 1749. [MdGaz#239]

DUNDAS, THOMAS, youngest son of John Dundas of Mannor, died in Reading, Pennsylvania, 1805. [AJ#3006]

DUNLOP, ALEXANDER, born 1739, son of William Dunlop a merchant in Virginia, matriculated at Glasgow University on 14 November 1752. [MAGU#47]

DUNLOP, JAMES, a merchant in Glasgow, then in North America 1769. [NAS.NRAS.0631.4]; a merchant in Canada, 1773. [NAS.GD1.151.1]; in Virginia 1771, [NAS.NRAS.0623.T-MJ, 327.5]; a merchant in Port Royal, Virginia, 1785, [NAS.GD1.850.43]; a merchant in Montreal 1784. [NAS.NRAS.0620.WC, bundle 4]

DUNLOP, JAMES, a merchant in Georgetown, Maryland,

1800. [NAS.CS17.1.19/53; CS26.910.60]; eldest son
of James Douglas the younger of Darnkirk, 1812.
[NAS.CS17.1.32/115]

DUNLOP, JAMES, in Petersburg, Virginia, 19 April 1801.
[NAS.RD5.402.628]

DUNLOP, JAMES, in Georgetown, Maryland, eldest son of
James Dunlop of Garnkirk, 1800, 1811.
[NAS.CS17.1.19/53; CS17.1.31/576]

DUNLOP, WILLIAM, a merchant in Greenock, later in
America, 1794. [NAS.CS17.1.13,308]

DUNLOP, WILLIAM, a merchant in Port Royal, Virginia,
1800. [NAS.CS17.1.18/414]

DUNSTER, CHARLES, formerly a servant to Lord
Strathallan, then in New Jersey, 29 April 1774.
[NAS.RS27.212.258]

EARNSHAW, JOHN, Collector of Customs on the James
River, Virginia, 1781. [NLS.Ch.3994]

EASON, PETER, Cardross, Dunbartonshire, emigrated from
Port Glasgow to St John, New Brunswick, on the
Favorite of St John, master John Hyndman, 22
October 1815. [PANB:MS.RS23E/f9798]

EASTON, DAVID, a merchant in Norfolk, Virginia, 1787.
[NAS.CS17.1.6/242]; also in 1806,
[NAS.CS17.1.25/466]

EDDIS, WILLIAM, and his wife Elizabeth, in Annapolis,
Maryland, 1776. [NLS.Ch.3939]

EDIE, JAMES, and his wife Marion Schaw, forgers,
sentenced to be tied to a cart-tail and whipped by the
hangman at all stations then to be taken to Glasgow,
there to be whipped before being transported to the

Plantations, 5 September 1739, [CM#3033]

EDWARD, ANDREW, in Bridge of Weir, to emigrate via
    Quebec to Upper Canada, 1820. [NAS.SC58.75.79]

ELLIOT, Mrs ELIZABETH, widow of Andrew Elliot, former
    Lieutenant Governor of New York, died in Edinburgh,
    1 May 1799. [AJ#2679]

ERSKINE, Sir WILLIAM, of Cambo, born in 1759, son of Sir
    Charles Erskine of Cambo and his wife Margaret
    Chiene, died at Niagara on 2 October 1791. [SP.V.93]

ESCHEARAGE, Major GEORGE, Westmoreland County,
    Virginia, was admitted as a burgess and guilds-brother
    of Ayr on 25 March 1729. [ABR]

EWING, EBENEZER, a merchant in Falkirk, Stirlingshire,
    now in Williamsburg, Virginia, 1789.
    [NAS.CS17.1.8/348]

EWING, ROBERT, in America, 1801. [NAS.CS17.1.20/416]

FAIRLIE, JAMES, a merchant in New York and Virginia,
    then from 1783 to 1796 in Kingston, Jamaica, later in
    Kilmarnock. [NAS.NRAS.00396.TD248.2]

FALCONER, JAMES, a rioter in Glasgow, husband of
    Margaret Miller, sentenced in 1725 to transportation to
    the colonies. [PRO.SP54.16.38/126]

FALCONER, WILLIAM, born 1736, feuar in Garmouth,
    former Governor of Severn Fort, Hudson Bay, died 1
    December 1801. [Essil gravestone]

FARQUHAR, JOHN, a planter in Jamaica, 1715.
    [NAS.RD4.117.589]

FARQUHAR, JOHN, surgeon's mate in Nova Scotia, 1749.
    [JCTP#57/112]

FARQUHAR, THOMAS, late a merchant in Edinburgh now in Virginia, 1782. [NAS.CS17.1.1/97]

FERGUSON, ARCHIBALD, a merchant in New England, third son of John Ferguson late baillie of Ayr, was admitted as a burgess and guilds-brother of Ayr on 17 September 1692. [ABR]

FERGUSON, ARCHIBALD, born 1795, a laborer in Callendar, emigrated from Port Glasgow to St John, New Brunswick, on the Favorite of St John, master John Hyndman, 22 October 1815. [PANB:MS.RS23E/f9798]

FERGUSON, DAVID, a merchant in Virginia, 1793/1795, eldest son of David Ferguson a merchant in Ayr and Customs Collector thereof. [NAS.CS17.1.12, 391; CS17.1.14/26]

FERGUSON, DOUGALD, a cooper from Greenock, in Georgia by 1801. [NAS.CS17.1.9/425]

FERGUSON, JAMES, in America 1799, 1805, eldest son of William Ferguson of Townhead, a merchant in Dumfries. [NAS.CS26.909.32; CS17.1.24/341]

FERGUSON, JAMES, eldest son of James Ferguson a merchant in Aberdeen, died in Halifax, Nova Scotia, 1817. [S.1.41]

FERGUSON, JOHN, in Virginia, 17.. [NAS.NRAS.0934, bundle 688]

FERGUSON, JOHN, a cooper from Greenock, in Georgia by 1801. [NAS.CS17.1.19/425]

FERGUSON, JOHN, born 1780, a laborer in Callendar, emigrated from Port Glasgow to St John, New Brunswick, on the Favorite of St John, master John

Hyndman, 22 October 1815. [PANB:MS.RS23E/f9798]

FERGUSON, JOHN, born 1794, a smith in Kincairn,
Perthshire, emigrated from Port Glasgow to St John,
New Brunswick, on the Favorite of St John, master
John Hyndman, 22 October 1815.
[PANB:MS.RS23E/f9798]

FERGUSON, N., late in Pennsylvania, now in Ayr, 1776.
[EUL.La.II.480,9]

FERGUSON, PETER, born 1795, a laborer in Stirling,
emigrated from Port Glasgow to St John, New
Brunswick, on the Favorite of St John, master John
Hyndman, 22 October 1815. [PANB:MS.RS23E/f9798]

FERGUSON, ROBERT, now in America, 1788.
[NAS.CS17.1.7/204]

FERGUSON, ROBERT, in North America 1805, eldest son
of Robert Ferguson of Castlehill 1805.
[NAS.CS17.1.24/455]

FINDLAY, CHARLES, born 1794, arrived in St John, New
Brunswick, in November 1815, on the Favorite of St
John, master John Hindman, from Scotland.
[PANB.MS.RS555/c4]

FINDLAY, JAMES, in Princeton, New Jersey, husband of
Anne, daughter of Robert Angus a merchant in
Kirkintilloch, 4 August 1775.
[NAS.RS10.Dunbarton.11.172]; Agnes Angus, spouse
of James Finlay now in America, 1788,
[NAS.CS17.1.7.8]; James Finlay, son of James Finlay,
merchant in Kirkintilloch now a weaver in Princeton,
New Jersey, and grandson of Robert Angus a
merchant in Kirkintilloch, 1790.
[NAS.RS.Dunbarton#514]

FINLAY, HUGH, Deputy Postmaster General of Quebec,

1780. [BL.Add.ms21,860]; 1784. [NAS.CS17.1.3/111]

FINLAYSON, JAMES, a merchant on the James River, Virginia, 1770, 1801. [NAS. CS17.1.9/233; CS18.708.4]

FINNIE, MARY, in Virginia, 1785. [NAS.CS17.1.4/345]

FINNIE, WILLIAM, Aberdeenshire, a Lieutenant of the 61st Company, 2nd Division, Royal Marines, died in Boston, pro. November 1775 PCC

FISHER, ADAM, a mariner in New York, son of James Fisher the Provost of Inveraray, 1772. [NAS.CS16.1.148/216]

FISHER, PETER, a bleacher in Rutherglen then in America 1805, only son of Alexander Fisher a farmer in Ditchmount. [NAS.CS17.1.24/244]

FLEMING, ROBERT, settled in Lanark, Upper Canada, by 1825. [BPP.2.167]

FLETT, THOMAS, at Severn, Hudson Bay, husband of Margaret Sinclair, 28 December 1789. [NAS.RS.Orkney#199]

FLUCKER, HANNAH, daughter of Thomas Flucker, late of Boston, New England, now in Edinburgh, 1787. [NAS.CC8.5.22]

FORBES, GEORGE, St Mary's County, Maryland, probate 16 June 1742, Prob.11/718 PCC

FORBES, JAMES, a merchant in New York, son of Dr James Forbes a physician in Aberdeen, died on passage from Savannah 26 September 1818. [AJ#3700][S#2/100]

FORD, WILLIAM, a merchant from Glasgow, now in Boston

1819. [NAS.CS17.1.38/267]

FORDYCE, CHARLES, Edinburgh, Captain of the 14th
Regiment of Foot, died in Virginia, pro. November
1777 PCC

FOREMAN, JAMES, a merchant in Halifax, Nova Scotia,
1822. [NAS.CS17.1.41/641]

FORRESTER, DAVID, from Forfar, Angus, a wright in
Canada, 1826. [NAS.RS.Forfar.7.73]

FORRESTER, JAMES, in Baltimore, Maryland, 1810.
[NAS.SC58.59.1.40]

FORSYTH, GEORGE, eldest son of William Forsyth in
Huntly, died in Niagara, Upper Canada, September
1806. [AJ#3072]

FORSYTH, WILLIAM, merchant in Halifax, Nova Scotia, co-
owner of the Lord Maccartney of Greenock, the
William of Greenock and the Cato of Greenock, 1798,
& the Liberty of Greenock 1800.
[NAS.CE60.5/187;11.6/17]

FOWLER, JAMES, a merchant in Virginia, 9 March 1703,
brother of Daniel Fowler, a merchant in Inverness.
[NAS.CS96.3309]

FRAME, JAMES, eldest son of Reverend James Frame in
Alloa, died in Petersburg, Virginia, 1803. [AJ#2921]

FRANCE, JOHN, in Pennsylvania, 20 June 1801.
[NAS.RD5.308.132]

FRASER, ALEXANDER or ANGUS, brother of William
Fraser of Balnain, in Mexico 1760s. [NAS.NRAS.0002]

FRASER, JAMES, Culmin, Kiltarlity parish, Inverness-shire,
paymaster of the Royal Artillery in New York, 1782.

[NAS.RS.Inverness#34]

FRASER, JAMES, son of James Fraser, a merchant in Barbados, 5 May 1790. [RGS.20.394]

FRASER, JAMES, in Detroit then in Aberdeen, testament confirmed on 14 November 1815 [NAS.CC1.6.W715]

FRASER, JAMES, born 1757, emigrated 1804, settled in Drummond, Pictou, Nova Scotia, died 1838. [Inverness Courier: 13 February 1839]

FRASER, JAMES, a merchant in Halifax, Nova Scotia, father of James De Wolf Fraser, 1824. [NAS.RS.Inverness#231/249]

FRASER, JOHN, Inverness, "brother to Fairfield", to America 1726. [Inverness Kirk Session Records: 22 February 1726]

FRASER, JOHN, a merchant in New York, 1782. [NAS.RS.Inverness#34]

FRASER, JOHN, a farmer in Dunwiddie County, Virginia, 1802. [NAS.CS17.1.21/470]

FRASER, JOHN, a surgeon in Windsor, Nova Scotia, probate 12 October 1819, Prob.11/1621 PCC

FRASER, PETER BISHOP, in Nova Scotia, 19 December 1829. [NAS.RD5.401.379]

FRASER, SIMON, merchant in Virginia, 1784. [NAS.CS17.1.3/375]

FRASER, SIMON, jr., a merchant in Quebec, son of Hugh Fraser of Dell, Inverness-shire, 1789. [NAS.RS.Inverness#275]

FRASER, SIMON, son of Alexander Fraser the Sheriff Clerk of Haddington, died in Gibsonport on the Mississippi River 23 October 1819. [AJ#3757][S.4.155]

FRASER, THOMAS, a planter late of South Carolina, died in Philadelphia, probate 17 July 1823, Prob.11/1673 PCC

FRASER, WALTER, in Dinwoodie County, Virginia 1816. [NAS.CS17.1.35/641]

FRASER, WILLIAM, in Nova Scotia, 1829, [NAS.RD5.401.379]

FREELAND, JAMES, husband of Jean Allan, in America 1800. [NAS.CS22.780.25]

FRENCH, JAMES, in Virginia 1784. [NAS.CS17.1.3/140]

FRENCH, WILLIAM, jr., late merchant in North America, 1804. [NAS.CS17.1.23/52]

FRIDGE, ALEXANDER, born in Elgin 1765, died in Baltimore, Maryland, 1838. [Inverness Courier: 13 February 1839]

FULTON, WILLIAM, in Louisville, Kentucky, 1824. [NAS.SC58.9.198]

GAILLARD, ESTHER, spouse of James Crockett in Charleston, South Carolina, 1750. [NAS.RD4.178.1.582]

GALBRAITH, WILLIAM, in America, 1819. [NAS.CS17.1.39/23]

GALLACHAN, JOHN, born 1792, arrived in St John, New Brunswick, 11.1815 on the Favorite of St John, master John Hindman, from Scotland. [PANB:MS.RS555/c4]

GALLOWAY, ROBERT, son of Andrew Galloway a

merchant in Glasgow, died in Fredericksburg, Virginia, 1.8.1794, [EA#3212]

GALT, WILLIAM, merchant in Virginia, 1820. [NAS.CS17.1.39/574]

GARDEN, WILLIAM, a gentleman in Pensacola, a witness to John Murray's deed, 18 February 1769. [NAS.RD4.205.1]

GARDINER, JAMES, a merchant in Augusta, Georgia, 1810. [NAS.CS17.1.30/551]

GARDINER, JOHN, an apprentice merchant in Edinburgh, a prisoner in Edinburgh Tolbooth, indented with Thomas Gardiner, a merchant in Edinburgh, for service in H.M. Plantations in America on 19 June 1744. [NAS.HH11/22]

GARDINER, JOHN, second son of Sylvester Gardiner MD in Boston, New England, matriculated at Glasgow University on 14 November 1752, graduated MA in 1755. [MAGU#46]

GARDNER, ANTHONY, King and Queen County, Virginia, 1789. [NAS.CS17.1.8/172]

GARDNER, DAVID, born in Montrose 1786, Assistant Commissary General of the Forces, died in St John, New Brunswick, 22 January 1827. [AJ#4135]

GARDNER, ROBERT, a merchant in Newburgh, America, 1794. [NAS.CS17.1.13,230]

GARNOCK, GEORGE, a shoplifter, banished to America for life, at Aberdeen March 1768, [AJ#1054]; whipped through Aberdeen while awaiting shipment to the Plantations in April 1768, [AJ#1056]; possibly transported on the George, master Peter Paterson, from Aberdeen to Virginia 25 May 1768. [AJ#1058]

GARNOCK, GEORGE, escaped from prison but recaptured, released from Edinburgh Tolbooth for transportation to the American Plantations 27.12.1768. [ETR/NAS.HH11/28]

GAY, WILLIAM, in Warwick, Virginia, 1773, son of John Gay senior in Port Glasgow. [NAS.RS81.9]

GEDDES, CHARLES, born in Edinburgh 1749, a watchmaker, died in Halifax, Nova Scotia, 27.9.1810. [EA#4926]

GEDDES, JOHN, in Virginia, son of William Geddes minister in Urquhart, 1720s. [NAS.RS29.V.210/262; RS29.VI.444/446]

GEDDES, WILLIAM, late a merchant in Philadelphia, 1795. [NAS.CS17.1.14,219]

GEIKIE, JAMES HENRY, and Catherine Amelia Gamble, had a daughter born 11 August 1807, baptised Catherine Carolina Eleanore 24 March 1811, on Colonel's Island, Glynn County, Georgia. [Arbroath Old Parish Register]

GEMMILL, ..., settled in Lanark township, Upper Canada, around 1820. [BPP.2.164]

GERARD, WILLIAM, Fredericton, New Brunswick, 1787. [NAS.GD1.768.16]

GIBSON, GEORGE, a weaver in Winchester, Virginia, 1818. [NAS.CS17.1.38/511]

GIBSON, JAMES, a merchant in Suffolk, Virginia, a benefactor under the will of Mr James Moir of Edgecombe County, North Carolina, 1761, [NAS.RD4.204.2]; 1769. [NAS.RS23.XX.372]; , of Kelton, late a merchant in Suffolk, Virginia, deceased by 1788. [NAS.CS17.1.7/111]

GIBSON, JOHN, a merchant in Virginia, eldest son of Robert Gibson a writer in Ayr, and Kilmarnock, Ayrshire, 1793, 1796. [NAS.CS17.1.12, 253; CS17.1.15/180]

GILCHRIST, JOHN, a merchant in Norfolk, Virginia, 1765. [NAS.GD180.629/2]

GILLES, DONALD, from Brunacovy, North Morar, emigrated on the brig Alexander of Greenock in June 1772, landed at Charlottetown, Prince Edward Island, 25 June 1772. [PAPEI#2664/138]

GILLESPIE, GEORGE, a planter in Bristol, Pennsylvania, probate 11 March 1782, Prob.11/1088 PCC

GILLESPIE, JAMES, born in Aberdeen 1787, died in Montreal 25.6.1821. [S.5.240]

GILLIES, JOHN, tenant of Lord MacDonald in Kendram, Skye, bound for America around 1802. [NAS.GD221.4433.1]

GILMORE, ROBERT, a merchant in Virginia, in London 1798. [NAS.CS17.1.17/15]

GILMOUR, JOHN MORTON, eldest son of Robert Gilmour deceased, a merchant sometime in Glasgow thereafter in Lancaster, Virginia 1799, 1800. [NAS.NRAS.0623.T-MJ, 427/68; CS17.1.18/138]

GILMOUR, ROBERT, formerly a merchant in Norfolk, Virginia, then in Glasgow 1782. [NAS.GD1.850.30]

GILMOUR, ROBERT, in Lancaster, Virginia, dead by 1788, husband of Helen, father of John and Robert, [NAS.CS17.1.7/233]

GLASSELL, JOHN, in Fredericksburg, Virginia, granted lands in Longniddry on 6 August 1779. [NAS.RGS.119/271][NAS.RS27.247.237]

GLEDSTONE, JOHN, a physician in Bermuda, probate 10 January 1811, Prob.11/1518 PCC

GLEN, ELIZABETH, born 15 February 1744, daughter of Reverend John Glen and Elizabeth Thomson in Forgandenny, Perthshire, married Dr George Johnson in Virginia 24 January 1772. [F.4.210]

GLENNIE, JAMES, in America, 24 May 1801. [NAS.RD4.272.176]

GLENNY, JAMES, a merchant in Canada, probate 20 May 1802, Prob.111/1374 PCC

GODFREY, GEORGE, born around 1738, an indentured servant who absconded from Captain William Tippell in Maryland in March 1753. [MdGaz#419]

GOLDIE, JAMES, emigrated from Dumfries to Virginia on board the Nannie and Jenny, master William Maxwell, 27 May 1749. [NAS.CS96.2161/9]

GOODAL, JANET, wife of Matthew Horsburgh, from Edinburgh, later in America, 1794. [NAS.CS17.1.13,96]

GORDON, ALEXANDER, from Aberdeen, a wright in Virginia 1787. [NAS.CS17.1.6/357]

GORDON, DAVID, merchant in New York, 1820. [NAS.CS17.1.39/602]

GORDON, GEORGE, in Bermuda before 1725. [NAS.GD44.43.16.128]

GORDON, JAMES, a merchant from Stromness, Orkney,

later in Savanna, Georgia, 1778.
[NAS.CS16.1.173/320; CS29.909.15]

GORDON, JAMES, in New York, dead by 1786, son of
James Gordon and Margaret Cruickshank.
[NAS.CS17.1.5/19]

GORDON, JOHN, born around 1724, an indentured servant
who absconded from Robert Perry, near Annapolis,
Maryland, on 14 September 1753. [MdGaz#438]

GORDON, JOHN, a merchant and trader in East Florida
1764-, later in Charleston, South Carolina, 1767.
[NAS.NRAS.771, bundles 403/489]; a merchant in
East Florida, 1776. [PRO.T1.522.44/5]; probate 31
March 1778, Prob.11/1163 PCC

GORDON, JOHN, Lancaster, Virginia, probate 27 April
1808, Prob.11/1477 PCC

GORDON, ROBERT, a merchant in Virginia then in
Glasgow, 1823. [NAS.RS54.1859]

GORDON, THOMAS, in New York, 1786.
[NAS.CS17.1.5/213]

GRACIE, WILLIAM, a merchant in Petersburg, Virginia, son
of the late William Gracie a merchant in Dumfries, died
in Glasgow on 25 April 1792. [GCr#104]

GRAHAM, GEORGE, alias Thomas Clunas, a convict
indentured servant, absconded from John Jordan,
Hugh Mitchell and Alexander Lothian in Charles
County, Maryland, on 12 January 1756. [MdGaz#560]

GRAHAM, GEORGE, a surgeon in Quebec, probate 18
December 1800, Prob.11/1351 PCC

GRAHAM, JOHN, died in Richmond, Virginia, 24
September 1820. [S.4.201]

GRAHAM, RICHARD, a merchant in Virginia, 1782.
[NAS.CS17.1.1/97]

GRAHAM, ROBERT, born 1782, son of Walter Graham in
Port Glasgow, died on Sullivan's Island, near
Charleston, 1802. [AJ#2852]

GRAHAM, SAMUEL, possibly from Glasgow, settled in
Maryland around 1771. [GM#IX.422.48]

GRAHAM, WILLIAM, a vintner in Quebec, probate 4 March
1780, Prob.11/1062 PCC

GRANT, ALEXANDER, born 1787, from Sutherland,
emigrated from Cromarty on the Ossian of Leith,
master John Hill, to Pictou in June 1821.
[IJ:29.6.1821]

GRANT, ARCHANGE, relict of Thomas Dickie in
Queenstown, Upper Canada, testament confirmed on
28 April 1829. [NAS.SC15.41.4.583]

GRANT, CUTHBERT, a merchant in Quebec, son of John
Grant a coppersmith in Inverness, and Naome
Cuthbert, 1790. [NAS.RS.Inverness#336]

GRANT, FRANCIS, at Fort Edward on 16 June 1758, and in
New York on 27 November 1758.
[NAS.GD248.47.1/81]

GRANT, HENRY, in Virginia 1812, eldest son of the late
Robert Grant a wine merchant in Leith, and grandson
of Robert Grant of Tillyfour. [NAS.CS17.1.31/336]

GRANT, JAMES, sometime in Montreal, natural son of
Cuthbert Grant, died in Portsoy on 10 August 1817.
[S.1.31][NAS.PS3.14/153]

GRANT, JOHN, a surgeon in Nova Scotia, 1754.

[NAS.CS96.1834, 3]

GRANT, JOHN, late a Lieutenant of the 42nd Regiment, with wife and family, in Urquhart, Inverness-shire, emigrated via Mull to New York on the Moore of Greenock, Captain MacLarty, July 1774. [AJ#1387]

GRANT, PATRICK, a merchant in Boston, sixth son of John Grant, Castlehill, Edinburgh, drowned in the wreck of the Esther sailing to Baltimore 20 November 1812. [AJ#3409]

GRANT, ROBERT, in Montreal, 30 July 1801. [NAS.RD3.298.535]

GRANT, THOMAS, in Virginia 1814. [NAS.CS17.1.34/456]

GRANT, WILLIAM, in Quebec 1767. [NAS.NRAS.771, bundle#414]

GRANT, WILLIAM, formerly a Lieutenant of the 42nd Regiment, with his wife and family, emigrated via Mull to New York on the Moore of Greenock, Captain MacLarty, 12 July 1774. [SM.36.446]

GRAY, ANDREW, son of William Gray of Gartcraig, died in Virginia 21.1.1802. [EA#3994]

GRAY, ANDREW, of Craigs, Dumfries-shire, died in Trenton, New Jersey, 22.9.1819. [EA#5838]

GRAY, Reverend **ARCHIBALD**, born 1763, minister of St Matthew's Church, Halifax, Nova Scotia, for 30 years, died 1826. [AJ#4112]

GRAY, HANNAH, wife of Jabez Pitt, in Accomack County, Virginia, 1786. [NAS.CS17.1.5/117]

GRAY, JOHN, merchant in Travellers Rest, Virginia, 1820. [NAS.CS17.1.39/622]

GRAY, RODERICK, late in Liverpool, son of David Gray of
Millbrae, died in Mobile, West Florida, 18 May 1820.
[EA#5907]

GRAY, WILLIAM, from Glasgow, then in Virginia 1787.
[NAS.RS.Glasgow#1602]; 1796. [NAS.CS17.1.15/231]

GRAY, WILLIAM, merchant in Virginia, eldest son of
William Gray, merchant there, and eldest son of Mrs
Isabella Bowie or Gray, 1820. [NAS.CS17.1.39/622]

GRAY, WILLIAM, born in Aberdeen, owner of the "Montreal
Herald", died 1822. [EEC#17292]

GREGORY, PETER MALLARDY, fourth son of William
Gregory merchant in Kilmarnock, died in Alexandria,
Virginia, 12.3.1817. [S.1.16]

GREIG, JAMES, a confectioner, died in New York 1805.
[AJ#2981]

GUINASH, JAMES, in Claching, Kintyre, to America on the
Diamond of Glasgow, master Robert Arthur, in 1740.
[NAS.SC54.48.14]

GUINASH, JOHN, in Claching, Kintyre, to America on the
Diamond of Glasgow, master Robert Arthur, in 1740.
[NAS.SC54.48.14]

HAIG, MAHAM, second son of George Haig a physician in
Charleston, South Carolina, matriculated at Glasgow
University in 1803, graduated MD there in 1807.
[RGG#243]

HALL, WILLIAM, a servant and a burglar, sentenced in
1736 to transportation to the colonies.
[PRO.SP54.22.45]

HALLIDAY, DAVID, a merchant in Petersburg, Virginia,

grant of Chapmanton on 5 July 1817.
[RGS.156.55.124]

HALLIDAY, GARDINER, JAMES, a merchant in Augusta,
Georgia, 1810. [NAS.CS17.1.30/551]

HAMBLETON, ARCHIBALD, an indentured servant who
absconded from the Bush River Iron Works, Maryland,
in March 1754. [MdGaz#473]

HAMILTON, ALEXANDER, in Maryland, 1782, 1787, eldest
son of the late James Hamilton of Kype, a writer in
Mauchline, Ayrshire. [NAS.CS17.1.1.425;
CS17.1.6/220]

HAMILTON, ALEXANDER, a merchant in Portobacco,
Maryland, died 30 June 1799. [AJ#2699]

HAMILTON, ARCHIBALD, of Overton, a merchant in
Virginia 1778. [NAS.CS16.1.173/162]

HAMILTON, BARR, in Virginia, 1794. [NAS.CS17.1.13,294]

HAMILTON, GEORGE, in Madison County Virginia, re
property in Fredericksburg 21.3.1803. [NAS.GD1.581]

HAMILTON, GEORGE LEWIS, Major of the Royal Artillery
in Quebec, probate 31 August 1801, Prob.11/1361
PCC

HANDASYDE, JAMES, surgeon's mate in Nova Scotia,
1749. [JCTP#57/112]

HAMILTON, JAMES, in Louden, Virginia, 1788.
[NAS.CS17.1.7,14]

HAMILTON, JOHN, in Nansemond, Virginia, 1765.
[NAS.NRAS.0620, GDB, bundle 2]

HAMILTON, JOHN, a merchant in Virginia 1778.

[NAS.CS16.1.173/162]

HAMILTON, JOHN, HM Consul in Virginia, probate 15 January 1817, Prob.11/1588 PCC

HAMILTON, JOHN, a wright and a wood merchant from Strathaven, now in America 1818. [NAS.CS17.1.38/365]

HAMILTON, MARY, born 1803, only daughter of Robert Hamilton in Quenton, Upper Canada, died in London 5.11.1823. [DPCA#1112]

HAMILTON, ROBERT, in America, ca1745. [NAS.NRAS.0560, bundle XIII]

HAMILTON, ROBERT, born 14 September 1753, son of Reverend John Hamilton and Jean Wight in Bolton, East Lothian, Member of the Legislature of Ontario, died 7 August 1777. [F#1.357]

HAMILTON, THOMAS, in Norfolk, Virginia, 1804. [NAS.NRAS.0620, GDB, bundle 2]

HAMILTON, WILLIAM, son of Reverend William Hamilton in Whitekirk, at the Palapsio River, Maryland, 24.8.1713. [NAS.RD2.103/2.527]

HAMILTON, WILLIAM, of West Quarter, a merchant in North Carolina, 1824. [NAS.CS17.1.44/50]

HANNAY, ROBERT, a merchant in St John's, Newfoundland, co-owner of the Northern Friend of Greenock, 1802. [NAS.CE60.11.7/9]

HARDIE, GEORGE, fifth son of Archibald Hardie a merchant in Bo'ness, died in Natchez, Georgia, 7 September 1818. [S#2/97]

HARDIE, THOMAS, in Norfolk, Virginia, 1764.

[NAS.RD3.224.347]

HARKNESS, PETER, in Montreal, 10 December 1823.
[NAS.RD5.310.361]

HARPER, WILLIAM, teacher at Albany Fort, Canada, 1805.
[NAS.NRAS.1861-63]

HARRISON, JOSEPH, Brownfield, Glasgow, Quartermaster
of the Loyal American Regiment, testament confirmed
on 3 September in1804 Glasgow. [NAS.CC9.7.76.6]

HART, BERTHA, in St Johns, New Brunswick, 1813.
[NAS.SC58.4.105]

HASTINGS, JOHN, Prestonpans, master of the James, died
in Virginia, probate September 1707 PCC

HAY, ALEXANDER, a merchant in Montreal, 1787.
[NAS.CS17.1.6/251]

HAY, HARRY, of Auchenstairs, in North America 1783.
[NAS.CS17.1.2/316]

HAY, JOHN, a surgeon in Surrey County, Virginia, son of
Robert Hay, maltman, portioner of Kirkintilloch, 8 April
1755. [NAS.RS.Dunbarton.8.462]

HAY, JOHN, sometime Customs Collector at Alloa now in
America, 1786. [NAS.CS17.1.5/27]

HAY, MARY, wife of James Milne, died in Pictou, Nova
Scotia, during 1807. [AJ#3095]

HAY, PETER, a boat-keeper at Petty Harbour,
Newfoundland, probate 23 March 1777, Prob.11/965
PCC

HAY, WILLIAM, a weaver from Glasgow, settled in
Dalhousie township, Upper Canada, around 1821.

[BPP.2.167]

HEADRICK, JOHN, sentenced in 1773 to transportation to the colonies. [PRO.SP54.46.91]

HENDERSON, ALEXANDER, youngest son of Reverend Richard Henderson the minister of Blantyre, matriculated at Glasgow University on 14 November 1748, died in Dumfries, Virginia, during January 1816. [SM#78.393][MAGU#39]

HENDERSON, ARCHIBALD, in Baltimore, Maryland, dead by 1814. [GA.T-ARD#13/1]

HENDERSON, DONALD, and his wife, from Eigg, emigrated on the brig Alexander of Greenock in June 1772, landed at Charlottetown, Prince Edward Island, 25 June 1772. [PAPEI#2664/155]

HENDERSON, JAMES, in New York, 1726. [NAS.RH9.1.221]

HENDERSON, JAMES, son of Archibald Henderson in Glasgow, died in Manchester, Virginia, 28 December 1799. [AJ#2719]

HENDERSON, JOHN, a staymaker in America, father of Thomas aged 3 who died in Aberdeen on 21 September 1784. [AU.MS2459]

HENDERSON, JOHN, late of Georgia, was granted lands of Broomhead on 2 February 1787. [NAS.RGS.124/82]

HENDERSON, NEIL, from Eigg, emigrated on the brig Alexander of Greenock in June 1772, landed at Charlottetown, Prince Edward Island, 25 June 1772. [PAPEI#2664/155]

HENDERSON, RICHARD, factor for John Glassford and Company of Glasgow in Bladenburg, Prince George

County, Maryland, 1766. [NAS.GD237/21/51, 15]

HENDERSON, ROBERT, died in York, Upper Canada, on 6
April 1812, {heir Christine, daughter of Walter Oswald
in Collessie Mill, Fife, sought in Scotland 1812},
[EA#5088]

HENDRY, DANIEL, in Charlotte County, Virginia, 1787.
[NAS.RS.Argyll#353]

HENRY, JAMES V., born 1797 in Albany, New York, arrived
in Liverpool on 4 December 1815, a gentleman,
residing at 21 Northumberland Street, Edinburgh.
[ECA.SL115.2.2/75]

HENRY, JOHN, a merchant from Aberdeen, died in Halifax,
Nova Scotia, 1 March 1813. [AJ#3407]; HENRY,
JOHN, born in 1779 second son of William Henry
(1744-1820) a weaver in Aberdeen and Margaret
Petrie (1744-1818), a merchant in Halifax, Nova
Scotia, died 1 March 1813. [St Nicholas gravestone,
Aberdeen]

HENRY, ROBERT JENKINS, a Maryland-Scot, a student at
Glasgow University in 1727. [MUGU#233]; was
admitted as a burgess and guilds-brother of Ayr on 14
May 1729. [AyrBR]

HEPBURN, THOMAS, born 1734, son of John Hepburn of
Urr, Dumfries-shire, and his wife Emilia Nisbet,
emigrated to Virginia around 1760, settled in Norfolk,
later in Port Royal on the Rappahannock River,
married Elizabeth Fox, father of Ann Thomas Hepburn
(1775-1838), a Loyalist in 1776. [TDG#23/235]

HERON, MARTHA, relict of James Maydman, Lieutenant of
an Independent Company in Bermuda, 1738.
[NAS.RD4.176/1.404]

HEUGH, ANDREW, a merchant in Virginia, 1787.

[NAS.CS17.1.6,94]

HIGHGATE, ROBERT, a wright in Parkersburg, Virginia,
son of James Highgate, a farm servant in Stewarton,
12 May 1845. [NAS.S/H]

HILL, JANET, a rioter in Glasgow, sentenced in 1725 to
transportation to the colonies. [PRO.SP54.16.38/126]

HILL, Reverend T., died in Montreal 14 March 1824.
[EEC#17592]

HILL, WILLIAM, died in New Orleans, 12 November 1826.
[AJ#4123]

HIND, JOSEPH, born 1785, a laborer in Port Glasgow,
emigrated from Port Glasgow to St John, New
Brunswick, on the Favorite of St John, master John
Hyndman, 22 October 1815. [PANB:MS.RS23E/f9798]

HISLOP, ROBERT, born 1785, a laborer in Port Glasgow,
with his wife Diana born 1783, and children James
born 1807, Mary born 1809, John born 1811, and
Jean born 1811, emigrated from Port Glasgow on the
Favorite of St John to St John, New Brunswick, 22
October 1815. [PANB:MS.RS23E/f9798]

HOGG, JAMES, a smith, sometime in North America, eldest
son of James Hogg a hammerman in Provan Mill,
1821. [NAS.CS17.1.40/219]

HOLBROOK, DIADEMA, in New York 6 June 1825.
[NAS.RD5.354.308]

HOLBROOK, ELEANOR, in New York 6 June 1825.
[NAS.RD5.354.308]

HOME, GEORGE, late of Great Black River, North America,
1784. [NAS.CS17.1.3/226]

HOME, JAMES, at Rappahannock Forge, Virginia, ca.1795.
[NAS.NRAS.0631.GD267#1-3]

HOME, PATRICK, at Rappahannock Forge, Virginia,
ca.1795.   [NAS.NRAS.0631.GD267#1-3]

HOOD, JOHN, a merchant in Flower d'Hundred, Virginia,
then in Greenock 1788, 1802. [NAS.CS17.1.7;
CS17.1.21/113]

HOOPE, UONY HAY, born 1790 in New York, landed at
Liverpool on 27 September 1807, a student of
medicine in Edinburgh. [ECA.SL115.2.2/63]

HOUSTON, JOHN, born 1743, son of John Houston a
merchant in Pennsylvania, matriculated at Glasgow
University in 1761, graduated from the University of
Pennsylvania in 1769, a surgeon of the Revolutionary
Army, died in Wrightville, York County, Pennsylvania,
on 5 June 1809. [MAGU#64]

HOWIE, JAMES, in Virginia 1796. [NAS.CS17.1.15/302]

HUIE, JAMES, jr., a shipmaster from Dumfries, then in
America, 1795. [NAS.CS17.1.14/123]

HUIE, PATRICK, a merchant in St Johns, Newfoundland,
son of James Huie sr. late merchant in Port Glasgow,
1819. [NAS.SC53.56.2/239]

HUME, CHARLES, only son of Dr George Hume, in
Jamaica, 1715. [NAS.RD4.117.295]

HUNTER, ADAM, in Fredericksburg, Virginia, 1775.
[NAS.GD1.384.23]

HUNTER, FRANCIS, born 1784 in Newport, Rhode Island,
arrived in Liverpool on 14 October 1805, a student of
medicine residing at Mrs Thomson's, Hay's Street,
Edinburgh, by October 1805. [ECA.SL115.2.2/47]

HUNTER, JAMES, an American student at Glasgow
University 1708. [MUG.189]

HUNTER, JAMES, a merchant in Virginia 1763.
[NAS.GD1.384.21]

HUNTER, JAMES, a merchant in Virginia, 1778.
[NAS.RS27.238.226]

HUNTER, J. S., in Charleston 10 May 1824.
[NAS.RD5.328.676]

HUNTER, JOHN, in America, third son of the late Mathew
Hunter a mason in Galston , 1808.
[NAS.CS17.1.27/320]

HUNTER, PATRICK, merchant in St John's, Newfoundland,
co-owner of the Northern Friend of Greenock, 1802.
[NAS.CE60.11.7/9]

HUNTER, PETER, a merchant in Newfoundland, co-owner
of the Hebe of Greenock, 1800. [NAS.CE60.11.6/72]

HUTCHISON, Mr JOHN, a prisoner in Edinburgh Tolbooth
1682, released, dead on arrival at Sandy Hook {New
Jersey?} 1684. [NAS/ETR]

HUTCHISON, Captain WILLIAM, Queens County,
Maryland, was admitted as a burgess and guilds-
brother of Ayr on 30 December 1704. [ABR]

HYSLOP, AGNES, spouse of David Gordon formerly in New
York now in Edinburgh, 1820. [NAS.CS17.1.39/438]

INGLIS, JOHN, in Philadelphia 1753.
[NAS.NRAS.0631.GDB, bdle. 4]

INGLIS, JOHN, from Carnwath, Lanarkshire, then in Fayette
County, Kentucky, now in Carnwath 1816.

[NAS.CS17.1.36/132]

INGRAM, JAMES, a merchant from Glasgow, later in
Virginia, 1798. [NAS.CS17.1.17/274]

INNES, ALEXANDER, a chaplain bound for the Leeward
Islands on 28 February 1694.[CTB#X.1.514]

INNES, LEWIS, or FARQUHARSON, a merchant in
Canada, second son of Alexander Farquharson of
Inverey, grant of Ballogie on 1 June 1816.
[RGS.153.32]

IRELAND, DAVID, a smith in Wigtown, with his wife and
family, emigrated to Pennsylvania 1773.
[PRO.T1/500/234]

IRELAND, JAMES, jr., son of James Ireland a writer in
Edinburgh, imprisoned in Edinburgh Tolbooth guilty of
shopbreaking in Edinburgh, released 3 September
1764 for transportation via Greenock to America.
[NAS.HH11/27]

IRVINE, ANDREW, educated at Theological Hall from 1806
to 1809, emigrated to America in 1809. [RPC#162]

IRVINE, JAMES, a merchant in Quebec, co-owner of the
Duke of Kent of Greenock, 1800, the Lord Keith of
Greenock, 1802, the Mary of Greenock, 1805.
[NAS.CE60.11.6/144; 7/6; 8/80/65]

IRVINE, JAMES, youngest son of James Irvine in Quebec,
died in Edinburgh 1 October 1820. [S.4.196]

IRVINE, Dr JOHN, late in Georgia, later in Enfield, England,
1792, 1798. [NAS.CS17.1.12, 78; CS17.1.17/11]

JACK, THOMAS, a merchant in Virginia, died at Airdrie
House, New Monklands parish, testament confirmed
22 September 1814 Commissariat of Hamilton.

[NAS.CC10.7.2.20; CS239.J14/2; CS96.4464-6]

JACKSON, WILLIAM, a merchant in Boston, 1806.
[NAS.CS17.1.25/363]

JAFFRAY, THOMAS, a tanner in St Ninian's, Stirling, then
in America, cnf 1798 Edinburgh

JAMESON, Dr ALEXANDER, of Bellmuir, graduated MD at
King's College, Aberdeen, 18 September 1742, settled
at Hampton on the James River, Virginia. [KCA.128]

JAMIESON, NEIL, a merchant in New York 1779.
[NAS.NRAS.0623.T-MJ.427/157]; born 1728, "long a
respectable merchant in Norfolk, Virginia", died in
London 20 May 1798. [AJ#2636]

JAMIESON, ROBERT, born 1791, arrived in St John, New
Brunswick, November 1815, on the Favorite of St
John, master John Hindman, from Scotland.
[PANB:MS.RS555/c4]

JARDINE, ROBERT S., Madison County, Virginia, probate
13 December 1815, Prob.11/1575 PCC

JEFFREY, THOMAS, a tanner in Stirling then in America,
testament confirmed 7 September 1798, Commissariat
of Edinburgh

JOHNSTON, ANDREW, a merchant in Virginia, dead by
1800. [NAS.CS17.1.19/113]

JOHNSTON, DANIEL, born 1764, late from White Bluff,
Savannah, Georgia, died in Leslie, Fife, on 4
December 1809. [PC#43]

JOHNSTON, DAVID, a tobacconist, eldest son of Thomas
Johnston a baker in Edinburgh, died in Savannah,
USA, 15 September 1820. [AJ#3818][S.4.215]

JOHNSTON, ROBERT, a merchant in Virginia, probate 5 April 1766, Prob.11/917 PCC

JOHNSTON, WILLIAM, a merchant from Glasgow, then in America, 1804. [NAS.CS17.1.23/301]

JOHNSTONE, WILLIAM, third son of James Johnstone a tanner in Glasgow, died in New York 1817. [S.1.34]

KEITH, ANDREW, a tenant in Garth, Caithness, imprisoned for housebreaking, theft and robbery, in Inverness Tolbooth and later in Edinburgh Tolbooth, released for transportation from Leith to Maryland on the Mally of Glasgow, Captain Peacock 20 September1769. [NAS.HH11/28]

KEITH, SKENE, late Brevet-Major of the 62nd Regiment, Bermuda, probate 18 May 1819, Prob.11/986 PCC

KELTIE, JOHN, a wright in America, 1816, grandson of John Keltie in Crook of Devon. [NAS.CS17.1.36/132]

KEMP, WILLIAM, born 1739, an indentured servant who absconded from John Glan, East Nottingham, Maryland, 2 July 1753. [MdGaz#428]

KENNAN, HENRY, a gentleman in Josephstown, Georgia, probate 9 March 1767, Prob.11/927 PCC

KENNAN, PATRICK, a merchant in America 1797. [NAS.CS17.1.16/376]

KENNAN, WILLIAM, an attorney in Richmond, Virginia, testament confirmed on 30 December 1768, Commissariat of Edinburgh. [NAS]

KENNEDY, ANGUS, son of Daniel Kennedy in Glasgow, died in St Lucie, Jamaica, 1802. [GkAd#75]

KENNEDY, ARCHIBALD, son of Daniel Kennedy in

Glasgow, died in Norfolk, Virginia, 1802. [GkAd#75]

KENNEDY, FRANCIS, Customs Collector of the Lower
James River District, Virginia, 1715. [NAS.GD27.5.14]

KENNEDY, HUGH, son of Daniel Kennedy in Glasgow, died
in Philadelphia, 1802. [GkAd#75]

KENNEDY, JAMES, son of Alexander Kennedy a cooper in
Virginia, apprenticed to Phin and Paterson merchants
in Edinburgh, for 5 years on 16 May 1798. [ERA]

KENNEDY, JAMES, a corporal of the Royal Scots in
Quebec, probate 31 July 1815, Prob.11/1570 PCC

KENNER, RODAMUS, an Anglo-Virginian student at
Glasgow University 1726. [MUG#230]

KENT, JOHN, born in Glasgow, a cabinet maker, arrived via
London in 1748, an indentured servant who
absconded from Matthew Hopkins, Rock Creek,
Prince George County, Maryland, on 19 September
1748. [MdGaz#178]

KEPPIE, GEORGE, born around 1722, a carpenter,
absconded from the Thomas, a snow, master Edward
Ogle in Severn, Maryland, on 13 January 1748.
[MdGaz#103]

KERR, ALEXANDER, prisoner in Edinburgh Tolbooth,
released for transportation to America 20 April 1764.
[NAS.HH#11/27]

KERR, EDWARD, in Virginia 1798, youngest grandson of
Edward Kerr a merchant in Irvine, Ayrshire.
[NAS.CS17.1.17/59]

KERR, GEORGE BROWN, in Newcastle, Hanover County,
Virginia, son of John Cunningham youngest brother of
Sir William Cunningham Fairlie of Robertland and

Fairlie, 1813. [NAS.CS17.1.34/362]; a merchant in Norfolk, Virginia, 1820. [NAS.CS17.1.39/491]

KERR, GEORGE, a merchant in Surrey, Virginia, 1792. [NAS.CS17.1.12,53]

KERR, JOHN, a servant, thief imprisoned in Dumfries Tolbooth, sentenced to be transported to America on 4 October 1722. [Dumfries & Galloway Archives: MS.GF4/19]

KERR, JOHN, a joiner from Thurso, Caithness, then in Baltimore, 1807. [NAS.CS17.1.26/140]

KERR, J. K., second son of William Kerr, surveyor General Post Office, Edinburgh, died in New York 1805. [AJ#3027]

KERR, MARGARET STEWART, wife of William B. Lamb, Norfolk, Virginia, 1820. [NAS.CS17.1.39/353]

KERR, MARIA, in Norfolk, Virginia, 1821. [NAS.CS17.1.40/216]

KERR, MARY, relict of James Fraser, Detroit, inventory dated 17 June 1820. [NAS.CC1.w967]

KERR, WILLIAM, in Manchester, Virginia, afterwards in Beith, testament confirmed on 6 January 1813 in Glasgow. [NAS.CC9.7.78.79]

KERR, WILLIAM, in Virginia, 28 January 1825. [NAS.RD5.320.403]

KEVAND, ALEXANDER, schoolmaster in Wickham, Queens County, New Brunswick, 1818. [NAS.RS.Wigtown.11248]

KEY, JAMES, a printer late in Philadelphia, in Edinburgh 1800. [NAS.CS17.1.19/33]

KINCAID, JOHN, sometime in Bellsdyke, then in North America, 1822. [NAS.CS17.1.41/647]

KING, JAMES, merchant in New York, deceased, 1789. [NAS.CS17.1.8/24]

KING, JAMES, in Bridge of Weir, to emigrate via Quebec to Upper Canada, 1820. [NAS.SC58.75.79]

KINNAIRD, JOHN FELDON, in Kent County, Maryland, 1819. [NAS.CS17.1.38/547]

KINNIBURGH, JOHN, sometime a wright in County Surrey, America, then in Kirkintilloch, 6 April 1752. [NAS.RS.10. Dunbarton.8.287]

KINNIBURGH, JOHN, a joiner in Sussex, Virginia, 1794. [NAS.CS17.1.13,40]

KIPPEN, J., a factor in Richmond, Virginia, 1764. [NAS.NRAS.0396.TD132.72]

KIRK, JAMES, son of James Kirk [1749-1829] and Elspeth Russell [1751-1832], a merchant in St Johns, New Brunswick. [St Andrews gravestone, Fife]

KIRK, WILLIAM, born in Dunfermline, Fife, 1746, served in the first American war, then settled in Pictou, Nova Scotia, died in St Mary's, Antigonish, 9 August 1843. [Scottish Guardian#1228]

KIRKPATRICK, THOMAS, a merchant in Alexandria, Virginia, brother of late William Kirkpatrick of Raeberry, 1782.[NAS.CS17.1.1.10/411]

KIRKWOOD, JAMES, a grocer from Glasgow, with his wife Cecilia Colquhoun, settled in America by 1806. [NAS.CS17.1.25/475]

KNOX, ROBERT, a merchant in Virginia, heir of John Knox a carpenter in Port Glasgow, 1782. [NAS.CD17.1.1.23]

KNOX, ROBERT DADE, in Wilkes County, Georgia, son of Robert Knox a merchant in Virginia, grandson of John Knox a shipwright in Port Glasgow, 1821, [NAS.CS17.1.40/183]; 13 March 1829. [NAS.RD5.398.456]

KYLE, JAMES, indented with James Corbet a merchant in Dumfries to serve in the American Plantations in 1728. [DGA.Misc.RB2/2/112, & GF4/19]

KYLE, JOHN, gardener in Kilbarchan, Renfrewshire, late a merchant on the St James River, Virginia, 1789. [NAS.CS17.1.8/347]

LAING, ANDREW, a writer from Edinburgh, now in America 1819. [NAS.CS17.1.39/323]

LAIRD, ANDREW, a baker from Greenock, then in America, eldest son of Hugh Laird a grocer in Crawforddykes, 1818. [NAS.CS17.1.38/29]

LAIRD, JAMES, born 1789, a laborer in Port Glasgow, emigrated from Port Glasgow to St John, New Brunswick, on the Favorite of St John, master John Hyndman, 22 October 1815. [PANB:MS.RS23E/f9798]

LAIRD, JOHN, son of William Laird a merchant in Port Glasgow, a merchant in Georgetown, Maryland, 1796, 1813, 1820. [NAS.CS17.1.15/419; NRAS.0623.T-MJ.353; SC58.59.3.211]

LAMB. ROBERT, a manufacturer from Glasgow, in America 1808. [NAS.CS17.1.27/344]

LAMB, ROBERT, from Hamilton, Lanarkshire, then in Fredericton, New Brunswick, 1815. [NAS.SC37.59.3/102]

LAMONT, ALEXANDER, tenant of Lord MacDonald in Brogaig, Skye, bound for America around 1802. [NAS.GD221.4433.1]

LAMONT, PATRICK BARRON, a painter, son of George Lamont in Aberdeen, died in New York 7 May 1828. [AJ#4199]

LANGWELL, WILLIAM, a dyer from Campbeltown, Argyll, settled in North America by 1800. [NAS.CS17.1.18/481]

LAURIE, JOHN, a miller from Strathmiglo, Fife, then in America 1809. [NAS.CS17.1.29/442]

LAURIE, WILLIAM, in Georgia 1814. [NAS.CS17.1.33/474]

LAWRIE, JOHN, son of Gavin Lawrie - Governor of East New Jersey, 1699. [NAS.RD2.82.418]

LAWSON, GAVIN, a merchant in Falmouth, Stafford County, Virginia, 1789, 1800. [NAS.CS17.1.8/347; CS17.1.18/384]; in Hampstead, Stafford County, Virginia, 1805, [NAS.CS17.1.24/15]; died in Geneva, Genessee, New York, 1805. [AJ#3003]

LAWSON, JOHN, in Nova Scotia 1809, son of Walter Lawson in Buckhaven, Fife. [NAS.B41.7.9]

LECKIE, ALEXANDER, late of New Providence, later in Virginia, 1808. [NAS.CS17.1.27/105]

LEE, Colonel PHILIP LUDWELL, of Westmoreland, Virginia, now living in Edinburgh, 1751. [EBR.MB#vi.165/6370]; was admitted as a burgess and guilds-brother of Ayr on 8 February 1751. [ABR]

LEECH, MATTHEW, adjutant of militia in Brockvill, Upper Canda, 1823. [NLS.Airth pp, ms10959, 154, 256]

LEES, JOHN, a mason in Canongate, Edinburgh, guilty of
perjury, released from Edinburgh Tolbooth for
shipment to America 15 March 1773.
[ETR/NAS.HH11/28]

LEGGAT, JOHN, a shipmaster in Water Street,
Philadelphia, cnf 15 June 1785 Edinburgh

LEISHMAN, ROBERT, born 1791, a laborer in Port
Glasgow, emigrated from Port Glasgow to St John,
New Brunswick, on the Favorite of St John, master
John Hyndman, 22 October 1815.
[PANB:MS.RS23E/f9798]

LEITCH, JAMES, a weaver from Glasgow, settled in North
Sherbrook township, Upper Canada, around 1821.
[BPP.2.167]

LEITCH, JOHN, sometime in Warwick, Virginia, now in
Parkhead, Holytown, 1783. [NAS.CS17.1.2.45]

LENNOX, DAVID, son of James Lennox in Kirkcudbright,
now in Kirkcudbright, late in Philadelphia, granted
lands of Port Mary on 2 February 1800.
[NAS.RGS.131/118]

LENNOX, ROBERT, in New York, 12 February 1829.
[NAS.RD5.387.745]

LENNY, JANET, late in Balfron now in America, 1819.
[NAS.CS17.1.39/23]

LESLIE, GEORGE, merchant in Quebec, co-owner of the
Duke of Kent of Greenock, 1800.
[NAS.CE60.11.7/144]

LESLIE, GEORGE, late a merchant in Edinburgh, died at
Cape Vincent, America, 7 May 1823.
[EEC#17509][DPCA#1105]

LESLIE, JOHN, in Florida, executor of James Duff who died in Jamaica, 1782. [AU.MS.2226/72/15]

LESLIE, JOHN, in Norfolk, Virginia, died 1819. [NAS.NRAS.0051]

LESLIE, ROBERT, a grocer from Burntisland, Fife, now in America,1810. [NAS.CS17.1.30/7]

LINKLETTER, WILLIAM, of the Hudson Bay Company, 6 August 1798. [NAS.RS.Orkney#426]

LIVINGSTONE, DONALD, with Jess, emigrated to Hudson's Bay on the Robert Taylor in 1812. [PAC.SP(C.1)560-562]

LIVINGSTONE, DUNCAN, with his wife, emigrated to Hudson's Bay on the Robert Taylor in 1812. [PAC.SP(C.1)560-562]

LIVINGSTONE, JOHN, a sorner imprisoned in Edinburgh Tolbooth, released on condition of leaving Scotland 5 March 1742. [NAS.HH11/21]

LIVINGSTONE, JOHN, a shoemaker, imprisoned in Edinburgh Tolbooth, indented with Thomas Gardiner a merchant in Edinburgh, for service in the American Plantations, 1744. [NAS.HH11/22]

LIVINGSTONE, MILES, emigrated to Hudson's Bay on the Robert Taylor in 1812. [PAC.SP(C.1)560-562]

LOCHHEAD, HENRY, a merchant in Alexandria then at the James River, Virginia, 1784; in Petersburg, Virginia, 1792. [NAS.CS17.1.3/354; CS17.1.12/15]

LOGAN, GEORGE, a merchant at Kemp's Landing, Princess Anne County, Virginia, and in Norfolk, Virginia, husband of Isabella ..., a Loyalist, died before

1783. [NAS.NRAS.0934.488]

LOGAN, WALTER, at Massachusetts Bay, 1771.
[NLS#Ch3872]

LOGAN, WALTER, Controller of Customs in Perth Amboy,
admitted as a burgess and guildsbrother of Glasgow,
as son of Reverend John Logan and Margaret
Murdoch in East Kilpatrick, 10 June 1784. [GBR]

LOMAX, LUNSFORD, an Anglo-Virginian student at
Glasgow University 1719. [MUG.217]

LOUDON-MCADAM, JOHN, a merchant in New York,
1782, son of James McAdam of Waterhead.
[NAS.CS17.1.1/286]

LOUTTIT, JOHN, of the Hudson Bay Company, grandson of
William Louttit in Lyking, Orkney Islands, 13 July 1808.
[NAS.RS.Orkney#755]

LOVE, ALEXANDER, a merchant in Virginia, 1799.
[NAS.CS17.1.18/364]

LOVE, JOHN, son of Allan Love, died at Poplar Mount,
Brunswick County, Virginia, on 6 April 1786.
[GM.IX.441.190]

LOW, ALEXANDER, in Virginia, second son of Alexander
Low a merchant in Falla deceased, 1787.
[NAS.CS17.1.6,380]

LOWELL, CHARLES, born 1782 in Boston, Massachusetts,
arrived in London during October 1804, a student of
theology residing at 6 Drummond Place, Edinburgh, in
1805. [ECA.SL115.2.2/45]

LUMSDANE, GEORGE, born 1789, a laborer in Callendar,
Perthshire, emigrated from Port Glasgow to St John,
New Brunswick, on the Favorite of St John, master

John Hyndman, 22 October 1815.
[PANB.MS.RS23E/f9798]

LUNAN, FRANCIS, a farmer, settled in East Florida 1767.
[NAS.NRAS.771, bundle 402]

LUNDIE, ARCHIBALD, a merchant in St Augustine, Florida,
trading to the Mississippi 31 October 1776.
[NAS.NRAS.0159.C4]

LYLE, JAMES, son of John Lyle a gardener in Kilbarchan,
Renfrewshire, deceased, a merchant on the James
River, Virginia, 1789. [NAS.CS17.1.8,347]

LYLE, JAMES, a merchant in Virginia, after in Meadowhead
of Strathblane, testament confirmed on 29 March 1813
in Glasgow. [NAS.CC9.7.78.144]

LYMBURNER, MATTHEW, merchant in Quebec, co-owner
of the Two Friends of Greenock, 1800.
[NAS.CE60.11.6/99]

LYON, ROBERT, a gentleman in Halifax, Nova Scotia,
probate 4 January 1821, Prob.11/1638 PCC

MCADAM, JOSEPH, a physician and surgeon at Corn
River, Northumberland County, Virginia, 1786,
possibly from Greenock. [NAS.RS81/12]

MCALESTER, ANGUS, in Lergyside, Kintyre, to America on
the Diamond of Glasgow, master Robert Arthur, in
1740. [NAS.SC54.48.14]

MCALESTER, DONALD, in Lergyside, Kintyre, to America
on the Diamond of Glasgow, master Robert Arthur, in
1740. [NAS.SC54.48.14]

MCALESTER, JAMES, in Dunalloch, Jura, to America on
the Diamond of Glasgow, master Robert Arthur, in
1740. [NAS.SC54.48.14]

MCALLISTER, JOHN, born 1796, a laborer in Greenock, emigrated from Port Glasgow to St John, New Brunswick, on the Favorite of St John, master John Hyndman, 22 October 1815. [PANB:MS.RS23E/f9798]

MCALLISTER, WILLIAM, late in Glasgow, now in America, 1803. [NAS.AC7/76]

MCALLUM, DANIEL, merchant in Virginia, 1784. [NAS.CS17.1.3/375]

MCALPINE, NEILL, in Knapp, to America on the Diamond of Glasgow, master Robert Arthur, in 1740. [NAS.SC54.48.14]

MCALPINE, WALTER, a bookbinder in Glasgow, later in America, 6 August 1776; 22 October 1776. [NAS.RS10.Dunbarton.11.256/278]

MACANDREW, DAVID, from Culross, later in America, 1824. [NAS.RS.Culross#1.40]

MCARTHUR, Captain NEIL, late of the Provincial Corps in America, now in Glasgow, 1789. [NAS.CS17.1.8/270]

MCAUSLAND, ROBERT, a merchant in Glasgow, later in Newfoundland, 1783, 1790. [NAS.CS17.1.2/212; CS17.1.9, 230]

MCBEATH, Mr, from America, admitted as a burgess of Elgin 1787. [Elgin Burgess Roll]

MCBRAIRE, JAMES, a merchant in Newfoundland then in Edinburgh, 1821. [NAS.CS17.1.40/231]

MCBRIDE, WILLIAM, in Maryland, 1804. [NAS.CS17.1.23/154]

MCCAEN, WILLIAM, a merchant in Virginia, 1778.

[NAS.CS16.1.173/159]

MCCALL, ARCHIBALD, late a merchant in Glasgow then in Virginia, 1788. [NAS.CS17.1.7/265]

MCCALL, JAMES, a merchant in Glasgow then in Virginia, testament confirmed on 14 April 1747 in Edinburgh. [NAS]

MCCALL, JOHN, late in Glasgow, then in New York, now in the West Indies, 1788. [NAS.CS17.1.7.17]

MCCALLUM, DUNCAN, born 1794, a laborer in Aberfoyle, emigrated from Port Glasgow to St John, New Brunswick, on the Favorite of St John, master John Hyndman, 22 October 1815. [PANB:MS.RS23E/f9798]

MCCALLUM, HUGH, in Lergyside, Kintyre, to America on the Diamond of Glasgow, master Robert Arthur, in 1740. [NAS.SC54.48.14]

MCCALLUM, JOHN, born 1791, a laborer in Gartmore, Perthshire, emigrated from Port Glasgow to St John, New Brunswick, on the Favorite of St John, master John Hyndman, 22 October 1815. [PANB:MS.RS23E/f9798]

MCCANDLISH, GEORGE, farmer in Wigtownshire, with his wife and family, emigrated to America 1773. [PRO.T1/500/234]

MCCAULL, WILLIAM, in Cothouse of Glenluce, a thief, banished to the American Plantations for 7 years, at Ayr 7 May 1766. [AJ#957]

MCCAW, JAMES, a physician in Virginia, son of William McCaw, a merchant in Newton Stewart 1787. [NAS.CS17.1.6/342]

MCCLELLAN, JOHN, Pennsylvania, was admitted as a

burgess and guildsbrother of Ayr on 4 June 1784.
[ABR]

MCCLURE, ALEXANDER, a merchant in St John,
Newfoundland, 1778. [NAS.CS96.1413, 8]

MCCOLL, JOHN, of Glassdrum, a merchant in Glasgow
then in New York, 1787. [NAS.CS17.1.5/115]

MCCORCIDALL, DONALD, in Gortansall, Jura, to America
on the Diamond of Glasgow, master Robert Arthur, in
1740. [NAS.SC54.48.14]

MCCORMIG, ANGUS, from Boisdale, South Uist, from
Boisdale, South Uist, emigrated on the brig Alexander
of Greenock in June 1772, landed at Charlottetown,
Prince Edward Island, 25 June 1772.
[PAPEI#2664/151]

MCCOUL, JOHN, in Fredericksburg, Rappahannock River,
Virginia, 1803. [NAS.CS17.1.22/349]

MCCRIMMAN, MALCOLM, from Kintail, emigrated from
Tobermory on the Emperor Alexander of Aberdeen,
master Alexander Watt, to Sydney, Cape Breton, in
July 1823, arrived there on 16 September 1823.
[IJ:30.1.1824]

MCCRIVAN, MALCOLM, in Balloachgerran, Lergie, to
America on the Diamond of Glasgow, master Robert
Arthur, in 1740. [NAS.SC54.48.14]

MACCULLOCH, DONALD, from Kintail, emigrated from
Tobermory on the Emperor Alexander of Aberdeen,
master Alexander Watt, to Sydney, Cape Breton, in
July 1823, arrived there on 16 September 1823.
[IJ:30.1.1824]

MCCULLOCH, THOMAS, a merchant in Virginia then in
Glasgow 1779. [NAS.NRAS.0623.T-MJ.363]

MCCURDY, JOHN, in America 1820, eldest son of Robert McCurdy a sailor in Saltcoats, Ayrshire. [NAS.CS17.1.39/489]

MCDIARMID, DONALD, born in Skye, died in South Carolina. [Inverness Courier: 5 February 1834]

MCDIARMID, JOHN, born 1791, a laborer in Kenmore, Perthshire, wife Isabella born 1788, emigrated from Port Glasgow to St John, New Brunswick, on the Favorite of St John, master John Hyndman, 22 October 1815. [PANB:MS.RS23E/f9798]

MACDONALD, ALEXANDER, from Morar, emigrated on the brig Alexander of Greenock in June 1772, landed at Charlottetown, Prince Edward Island, 25 June 1772. [PAPEI/2664/71, 144, 147]

MACDONALD, ALEXANDER, from Eigg, emigrated on the brig Alexander of Greenock in June 1772, landed at Charlottetown, Prince Edward Island, 25 June 1772. [PAPEI#2664/142]

MACDONALD, ALLAN, from Kintail, emigrated from Tobermory on the Emperor Alexander of Aberdeen, master Alexander Watt, to Sydney, Cape Breton, in July 1823, arrived there on 16 September 1823. [IJ:30.1.1824]

MACDONALD, ALLAN, from South Uist, emigrated from Tobermory on the Emperor Alexander of Aberdeen, master Alexander Watt, to Sydney, Cape Breton, in July 1823, arrived there on 16 September 1823. [IJ:30.1.1824]

MACDONALD, ANGUS, from Cornua, emigrated on the brig Alexander of Greenock in June 1772, landed at Charlottetown, Prince Edward Island, 25 June 1772. [PAPEI#2664/149, 139]

MCDONALD, ANGUS, from Boisdale, South Uist, from Boisdale, South Uist, emigrated on the brig Alexander of Greenock in June 1772, landed at Charlottetown, Prince Edward Island, 25 June 1772. [PAPEI#2664/151]

MCDONALD, ANGUS, with his family of seven, from Druimindarroch, Inverness-shire, emigrated from there aboard the Jane, Captain Fisher, to Prince Edward Island in July 1790. [SCA]

MCDONALD, ANGUS, and family, emigrated from Greenock to New York on the Frances of New Orleans in 1812, to settle in Highlandtown, Columbiana County, Ohio. [SHR#63/53]

MCDONALD, ANGUS, born 1767, his wife Mary McLugash, born 1772, with children Donald born 1794, a laborer, Jean born 1796, Anne born 1798, Archibald born 1798, and Alexander born 1804, in Balinhard, Kilfinichen, Mull, emigrated to Hudson Bay in 1812. [NAC.SP(C1), 294, 558-61]

MACDONALD, ANGUS, from North Uist, emigrated from Tobermory on the Emperor Alexander of Aberdeen, master Alexander Watt, to Sydney, Cape Breton, in July 1823, arrived there on 16 September 1823. [IJ:30.1.1824]

MACDONALD, ARCHIBALD, from Badenoch, emigrated from Tobermory on the Emperor Alexander of Aberdeen, master Alexander Watt, to Sydney, Cape Breton, in July 1823, arrived there on 16 September 1823. [IJ:30.1.1824]

MCDONALD, AUGUSTIN, in Pictou, Nova Scotia, 1802. [SCA.BL/4/187/16]

MACDONALD, CHRISTIAN, from South Uist, emigrated

from Tobermory on the Emperor Alexander of Aberdeen, master Alexander Watt, to Sydney, Cape Breton, in July 1823, arrived there on 16 September 1823. [IJ:30.1.1824]

MCDONALD, DONALD, Lewis, a prisoner in Tain Tolbooth, a bigamist in Tarbert, was transported to America 1767. [Tain document #259 in Old Ross-shire and Scotland, W. McGill, Inverness, 1909, p.97]

MCDONALD, DONALD, from Bornish, South Uist, emigrated on the brig Alexander of Greenock in June 1772, landed at Charlottetown, Prince Edward Island, 25 June 1772, settled at Scotchfort. [PAPEI#2664/153]

MCDONALD, DONALD, from Borrodale, emigrated on the brig Alexander of Greenock in June 1772, landed at Charlottetown, Prince Edward Island, 25 June 1772, settled at Portage. [PAPEI#2664/153]

MCDONALD, DONALD, with his family of five, from Armadale, Sleat, emigrated from Druimindarroch, Inverness-shire, aboard the Jane, Captain Fisher, bound for Prince Edward Island in July 1790. [SCA]

MCDONALD, DONALD, born 1805, with his family of one, from Sutherland, emigrated from Cromarty on the Ossian of Leith, master John Hill, to Pictou in June 1821. [IJ:29.6.1821]

MACDONALD, DONALD, from South Uist, emigrated from Tobermory on the Emperor Alexander of Aberdeen, master Alexander Watt, to Sydney, Cape Breton, in July 1823, arrived there on 16 September 1823. [IJ:30.1.1824]

MACDONALD, Captain G., at Fort George, Niagara, Upper Canada, 1820. [SCA.OL/6/8/11]

MCDONALD, GEORGE, born 1790, a laborer in Falkirk, Stirlingshire, emigrated from Port Glasgow to St John, New Brunswick, on the Favorite of St John, master John Hyndman, 22 October 1815. [PANB.MS.RS23E/f9798]

MACDONALD, JAMES, born 1736, Catholic priest, from Moidart, emigrated on the brig Alexander of Greenock in June 1772, landed at Charlottetown, Prince Edward Island, 25 June 1772. [SCA.BL3.242/2; BL/3/288/9, 10]

MCDONALD, JOHN, from Stonybridge, from Boisdale, South Uist, emigrated on the brig Alexander of Greenock in June 1772, landed at Charlottetown, Prince Edward Island, 25 June 1772. [PAPEI#2664/151]

MCDONALD, JOHN, a merchant in Montreal, 1798. [NAS.CS96/608]

MCDONALD, JOHN, with his family of three, from Ardnish, Arisaig, Inverness-shire, emigrated from Druimindarroch, Inverness-shire, aboard the Jane, Captain Fisher, bound for Prince Edward Island in July 1790. [SCA]

MACDONALD, JOHN, tenant of Lord MacDonald in Balmacqueen, Skye, bound for America around 1802. [NAS.GD221.4433.1]

MACDONALD, JOHN, tenant of Lord MacDonald in Peigown and Osmigarry, Skye, bound for America around 1802. [NAS.GD221.4433.1]

MACDONALD, JOHN, from Arisaig, emigrated from Tobermory on the Emperor Alexander of Aberdeen, master Alexander Watt, to Sydney, Cape Breton, in July 1823, arrived there on 16 September 1823. [IJ:30.1.1824]

MCDONALD, JOHN, in Antigonish, Nova Scotia, 1826.
[SCA.OL/6/12/13]

MCDONALD, LAUGHLIN, born in the Highlands, a soldier
in Loudon's Highlanders, in Boston 1757, at
Louisbourg 1758, at the Plains of Abraham and the
Siege of Quebec, fought under Admiral Hawke in the
West Indies, died in Belfast, USA, 25 August 1821.
[S.5.247]

MACDONALD, MALCOLM, from North Uist, emigrated from
Tobermory on the Emperor Alexander of Aberdeen,
master Alexander Watt, to Sydney, Cape Breton, in
July 1823, arrived there on 16 September 1823.
[IJ:30.1.1824]

MCDONALD, Mrs MARGARET, born 1761, a widow with
her family of four, from Sutherland, emigrated from
Cromarty on the Ossian of Leith, master John Hill, to
Pictou in June 1821. [IJ:29.6.1821]

MACDONALD, RANALD, from Alassay, emigrated on the
brig Alexander of Greenock in June 1772, landed at
Charlottetown, Prince Edward Island, 25 June 1772.
[PAPEl#2664/ 141, 149, 139]

MCDONALD, RANALD, from Boisdale, South Uist, from
Boisdale, South Uist, emigrated on the brig Alexander
of Greenock in June 1772, landed at Charlottetown,
Prince Edward Island, 25 June 1772.
[PAPEl#2664/151]

MCDONALD, RODERICK, a tenant farmer from Glenuig,
Inverness-shire, and his family of five, emigrated from
Druimindarroch, Inverness-shire, aboard the Jane,
Captain Fisher, bound for Prince Edward Island in July
1790. [SCA]

MCDONALD, WILLIAM, born 1766, with his family of ten,

from Sutherland, emigrated from Cromarty on the
Ossian of Leith, master John Hill, to Pictou in June
1821. [IJ:29.6.1821]

MCDONELL, AENEAS, late Captain of the 6th Royal
Veterans, died in Nelson, Miramachi, 10 March 1828.
[AJ#4205]

MCDONELL, ALEXANDER, in Canada, 1812.
[SCA.PL/3/35/11]

MCDONELL, Reverend ALEXANDER, in Upper Canada,
1819. [SCA.OL/6/7/9]

MCDONELL, CHARLES, late Captain of Fraser's
Highlanders, probate 24 November 1763,
Prob.11/893, PCC

MCDONOUGH, THOMAS, British Consul in Massachusetts,
died in Boston 1805. [AJ#2986]

MCDOUALL, JOHN, brother of the Earl of Dumfries, a
merchant in Virginia, a Loyalist in 1778.
[NAS.NRAS.0631.GDB.4]

MCDOUGAL, DOUGAL, born 1785, a laborer in Greenock,
emigrated from Port Glasgow to St John, New
Brunswick on the Favorite of St John, master John
Hyndman, 22 October 1815. [PANB:MS.ES23E/f9798]

MCDOUGALL, ALEXANDER, late tacksman of Achtemmy,
Ardnamurchan, and his family, emigrated on the
Louisa of Aberdeen 28 July 1819, landed in Pictou,
Nova Scotia, 31 August 1819. [EA#5813/5832#]

MACDOUGALL, MALCOLM, from Barra, emigrated from
Tobermory on the Emperor Alexander of Aberdeen,
master Alexander Watt, to Sydney, Cape Breton, in
July 1823, arrived there on 16 September 1823.
[IJ:30.1.1824]

MCDOWAL, ..., to Florida as an estate manager 1766. [NAS.NRAS.771, bundle 295]

MCDOWALL, PATRICK, a merchant, formerly in Virginia, 1755. [NAS.RS23.XVII.337]

MCEACHERN, AENEAS B., a Catholic bishop, St Andrew's, Prince Edward Island, 1819. [SCA.BL/5/59/7, 18]

MCEACHERN, ANGUS, at Savage Harbour, Canada, 1791. [SCA.BL/4/33/11]

MACEACHERN, DONALD, son of Ewan MacEachern, from Kinlochmoidart, emigrated on the brig Alexander of Greenock in June 1772, landed at Charlottetown, Prince Edward Island, 25 June 1772. [PAPEI#2664/71, 144, 147]

MACEACHERN, EWAN, from Kinlochmoidart, emigrated on the brig Alexander of Greenock in June 1772, landed at Charlottetown, Prince Edward Island, 25 June 1772. [PAPEI.2664/70, 150]

MACEACHERN, HUGH BAN, from Kinlochmoidart, emigrated on the brig Alexander of Greenock in June 1772, landed at Charlottetown, Prince Edward Island, 25 June 1772. [PAPEI#2664/153]

MCEARLICH, JOHN, from Kintail, emigrated from Tobermory on the Emperor Alexander of Aberdeen, master Alexander Watt, to Sydney, Cape Breton, in July 1823, arrived there on 16 September 1823. [IJ:30.1.1824]

MCEWAN, JOHN, born 1796, a laborer in Dunbarton, emigrated from Port Glasgow to St John, New Brunswick, on the Favorite of St John, master John Hyndman, 22 October 1815. [PANB.MS.RS23E/f9798]

MCFALL, JAMES, born around 1713, an indentured servant who absconded from Margaret Urie in Bladensburg, 18 July 1753. [MdGaz#434]

MCFARLANE, ALEXANDER, born 1790, a laborer in Callendar, emigrated from Port Glasgow to St John, New Brunswick, on the Favorite of St John, master John Hyndman, 22 October 1815. [PANB:MS.RS23E/f9798]

MCFARLANE, ANDREW, of Blairnerne, sometime a merchant in New York, husband of Elizabeth Cumming, 3 September 1755. [NAS.RS10.Dunbarton.3.501]

MCFARLANE, DUNCAN, born 1782, a laborer in Strathfillan, Perthshire, emigrated from Port Glasgow to St John, New Brunswick, on the Favorite of St John, master John Hyndman, 22 October 1815. [PANB.MS.RS23E/f9798]

MCFIE, DONALD, emigrated on the brig Alexander of Greenock in June 1772, landed at Charlottetown, Prince Edward Island, 25 June 1772. [SCA.BL3.247/7]

MCFREDERICK, EDWARD, son of the late William McFrederick, saddler at Saddler's Crossroads, Queen Anne County, Maryland, 1810. [NAS.CS17.1.30/366]

MCFREDERICK, ROBERT, son of the late William McFrederick, saddler at Saddler's Crossroads, Queen Anne County, Maryland, 1810. [NAS.CS17.1.30/366]

MCGAW, JAMES, late a merchant in Alexandria, America, now in Scotland, 1798. [NAS.CS17.1.17/367]

MCGILL, JAMES, in Montreal, probate 24 August 1814, Prob.11/1559 PCC

MCGILL, JOHN, a merchant in Montreal, died there 1 December 1797. [AJ#2615]

MCGILLVRAY, JOHN, with his family of five, from Marney, Arisaig, Inverness-shire, emigrated from Druimindarroch, Inverness-shire, aboard the Jane, Captain Fisher, bound for Prince Edward Island in July 1790. [SCA]

MCGILLVRAY, Lieutenant Colonel **JOHN**, in Georgia, 1789, 1790. [NAS.RS.Ross & Cromarty#74/296]

MCGILLVRAY, WILLIAM, in Montreal, was granted the lands of Broloss on 2 June 1819. [NAS.RGS.159.24.42]; husband of Magdalene Macdonald, 5 October 1820. [NAS.RS.Argyll#3205]

MCGLASHAN, ADAM, a merchant in Newfoundland then in Glasgow, 1801. [NAS.RS.Ross & Cromarty#130]

MCGRAW, ALEXANDER, possibly from Moidart, emigrated on the brig Alexander of Greenock in June 1772, landed at Charlottetown, Prince Edward Island, 25 June 1772. [SCA.BL3.242/2]

MCGRAW, DANIEL, a Highland indentured servant, absconded from Fredericksburg on 20 July 1746. [MdGaz#76]

MCGREGOR, ALEXANDER, born 1794, a surgeon in Edinburgh, emigrated from Port Glasgow to St John, New Brunswick, on the Favorite of St John, master John Hyndman, 22 October 1815. [PANB:MS.RS.23E/f9798]

MCGREGOR, DONALD, born 1781, a laborer in Callendar, emigrated from Port Glasgow to St John, New Brunswick, on the Favorite of St John, master John Hyndman, 22 October 1815. [PANB:MS.RS23E/f9798]

MCGREGOR, DONALD, born 1777, Doune, Stirlingshire, with his wife Agnes born 1788, and children William born 1801 a laborer, Mary born 1803 a servant, Agnes born 1805, Elizabeth born 1807, Grizel born 1810, and Jane born 1812, emigrated from Port Glasgow to St John, New Brunswick, on the Favorite of St John, master John Hyndman, 22 October 1815. [PANB:MS,RS23E/f9798]

MCGREGOR, DUNCAN, born 1775, a laborer in Callendar, Perthshire, with wife Janet born 1776, and children Catherine born 1795, Margaret born 1797 a servant, Gregor born 1798 a laborer, Isabella born 1800 a servant, Mary born 1801, Marjorie born 1803, James born 1809, and Elizabeth born 1809, emigrated from Port Glasgow to St John, New Brunswick, on the Favorite of St John, master John Hyndman, 22 October 1815. [PANB:MS.RS23E/f9798]

MCGREGOR, JAMES, born 1775, a laborer in Strathyre, Balquhidder, wife Margaret born 1777, children Elizabeth born 1800, Janet born 1802, William born 1804, Colin born 1805, John born 1812, and James born 1813, emigrated from Port Glasgow to St John, New Brunswick, on the Favorite of St John, master John Hyndman, 22 October 1815. [PANB:MS.RS23E/f9798]

MCGREGOR, JAMES, born 1800, a laborer in Callendar, Perthshire, emigrated from Port Glasgow to St John, New Brunswick, on the Favorite of St John, master John Hyndman, 22 October 1815. [PANB:MS.RS23E/f9798]

MCGREGOR, JOHN, a merchant in New York, died in Govanbank, Glasgow, 1802. [AJ#2851]

MCGREGOR, JOHN, late in Imracrioch, later in America, 1804. [NAS.CS17.1.23/235]

MCGREGOR, JOHN, born 1794, a laborer in Callendar, emigrated from Port Glasgow to St John, New Brunswick, on the Favorite of St John, master John Hyndman, 22 October 1815. [PANB:MS.RS23E/f9798]

MCGREGOR, PETER, born 1781, a laborer in Callendar, Perthshire, emigrated from Port Glasgow to St John, New Brunswick, on the Favorite of St John, master John Hyndman 22 October 1815. [PANB:MS.RS23E/f9798]

MCGREGOR, PETER, born 1813, Callendar, Perthshire, emigrated from Port Glasgow to St John, New Brunswick, on the Favorite of St John, master John Hyndman, 22 October 1815. [PANB:MS.RS23E/f9798]

MCGRIGOR, DONALD GLASS, a prisoner in Finlarig, Breadalbane, sentenced to be sent to the 'foreign plantations never to return', in 1683. [NAS.GD112/17/1/7/17]

MCGRIGOR, EVAN, farm servant in New Milne, a prisoner in Inverness 1709, transported to America. ["Old Ross-shire and Scotland" p.97]

MCGRORIE, JANE, wife of Dr Suther, Royal Navy, died in Truro, Nova Scotia, 10 July 1823. [DPCA#1100]

MCGURDY, DANIEL, born 1793, arrived in St John, New Brunswick, during November 1815, on the Favorite of St John, master John Hindman, from Scotland. [PANB.MS.RS555/c4]

MCHARDY, WILLIAM, born 1797, eldest son of Mr McHardy schoolmaster of Fetteresso, died in Savannah 22 September 1820. [AJ#3800]

MCHWOIL. DONALD, a cowstealer, who was banished to the Plantations, at Inverness in May 1751. [SHR.20.251]

MCHWOIL, or MCMILLAN, NEIL, a cowstealer, who was banished to the Plantations, at Inverness in May 1751. [SHR.20.251]

MCILBRIDE, ANGUS, to America on the Diamond of Glasgow, master Robert Arthur, in 1740. [NAS.SC54.48.14]

MCILBRIDE, ARCHIBALD, in Dunalloch, to America on the Diamond of Glasgow, master Robert Arthur, in 1740. [NAS.SC54.48.14]

MCILBRIDE, NEIL, in Dunalloch, to America on the Diamond of Glasgow, master Robert Arthur, in 1740. [NAS.SC54.48.14]

MCILLEHALLUM, KATHRINE, in Lergysides, to America on the Diamond of Glasgow, master Robert Arthur, in 1740. [NAS.SC54.48.14]

MCINNIS, DUNCAN, from Boisdale, South Uist, emigrated on the brig Alexander of Greenock in June 1772, landed at Charlottetown, Prince Edward Island, 25 June 1772. [PAPEI#2664/151]

MACINNIS, DONALD, from Barra, emigrated on the brig Alexander of Greenock in June 1772, landed at Charlottetown, Prince Edward Island, 25 June 1772. [PAPEI#2664/151]

MCINNES, ..., a mason, emigrated on the brig Alexander of Greenock in June 1772, landed at Charlottetown, Prince Edward Island, 25 June 1772. [SCA.BL3.248/1]

MCINNISH, ANGUS, of Ardlussa, Jura, to America on the Diamond of Glasgow, Captain Robert McArthur, in 1740. [NAS.SC51.48.14]

MCINNISH, DONALD, of Ardmenish, Jura, to America on

the Diamond of Glasgow, Captain Robert McArthur, in 1740. [NAS.SC51.48.14]

MCINTOSH, DONALD, from Boisdale, South Uist, from Boisdale, South Uist, emigrated on the brig Alexander of Greenock in June 1772, landed at Charlottetown, Prince Edward Island, 25 June 1772. [PAPEI#2664/151]

MCINTOSH, DUNCAN, Lieutenant Colonel of the 60th Regiment, Quebec, probate 20 July 1815, Prob.11/1570 PCC

MCINTOSH, JAMES, son of William McIntosh, arrived in New York 26 July 1775, settled in West Chester near New York as a schoolmaster. [NAS.GD248.508.4.71]

MCINTOSH, JOHN, a sailor in Leith, imprisoned in Edinburgh Tolbooth for housebreaking in Leith, released 23 September 1764 to be transported via Greenock to America. [NAS.HH11/27]

MACINTOSH, PETER, born 1727, a farmer and indentured servant who absconded from John Stansbury, Patapsco Forest, Baltimore County, Maryland, on 28 July 1754. [MdGaz#482]

MCINTOSH, WILLIAM, released from Edinburgh Tolbooth for shipment to America via Glasgow on 24 January 1775. [NAS.HH11/28]

MCINTOSH, WILLIAM, son of William McIntosh, arrived in New York on 26 July1775. [NAS.GD248.508.4.71]

MACINTYRE, ALEXANDER, from South Uist, emigrated from Tobermory on the Emperor Alexander of Aberdeen, master Alexander Watt, to Sydney, Cape Breton, in July 1823, arrived there on 16 September 1823. [IJ:30.1.1824]

MCINTYRE, ANGUS, from Barra, emigrated on the brig
Alexander of Greenock in June 1772, landed at
Charlottetown, Prince Edward Island, 25 June 1772.
[PAPEI#2664/151]

MACINTYRE, ANGUS, from South Uist, emigrated from
Tobermory on the Emperor Alexander of Aberdeen,
master Alexander Watt, to Sydney, Cape Breton, in
July 1823, arrived there on 16 September 1823.
[IJ:30.1.1824]

MACINTYRE, ANGUS, from Benbecula, emigrated from
Tobermory on the Emperor Alexander of Aberdeen,
master Alexander Watt, to Sydney, Cape Breton, in
July 1823, arrived there on 16 September 1823.
[IJ:30.1.1824]

MACINTYRE, DUNCAN, from Benbecula, emigrated from
Tobermory on the Emperor Alexander of Aberdeen,
master Alexander Watt, to Sydney, Cape Breton, in
July 1823, arrived there on 16 September 1823.
[IJ:30.1.1824]

MACINTYRE, EFFIE, from South Uist, emigrated from
Tobermory on the Emperor Alexander of Aberdeen,
master Alexander Watt, to Sydney, Cape Breton, in
July 1823, arrived there on 16 September 1823.
[IJ:30.1.1824]

MCINTYRE, JOHN, from Boisdale, South Uist, emigrated on
the brig Alexander of Greenock in June 1772, landed
at Charlottetown, Prince Edward Island, 25 June 1772.
[PAPEI#2664/151]

MCINTYRE, JOHN, from Barra, emigrated on the brig
Alexander of Greenock in June 1772, landed at
Charlottetown, Prince Edward Island, 25 June 1772.
[PAPEI#2664/148]

MACINTYRE, JOHN, from South Uist, emigrated from

Tobermory on the Emperor Alexander of Aberdeen, master Alexander Watt, to Sydney, Cape Breton, in July 1823, arrived there on 16 September 1823. [IJ:30.1.1824]

MCINTYRE, MALCOLM, born 1779, a laborer in Callendar, Perthshire, emigrated from Port Glasgow to St John, New Brunswick, on the Favorite of St John, master John Hyndman, 22 October 1815. [PANB:MS.RS23E/f9798]

MCINTYRE, NEIL, from Barra, emigrated on the brig Alexander of Greenock in June 1772, landed at Charlottetown, Prince Edward Island, 25 June 1772. [PAPEI#2664/156]

MCINTYRE, PETER, born 1782, a laborer in Callendar, Perthshire, wife Isabella born 1782, children Jean born 1809, John born 1811, and Janet born 1813, emigrated from Port Glasgow to St John, New Brunswick, on the Favorite of St John, master John Hyndman, on 22 October 1815. [PANB:MS.RS23E/f9798]

MCINTYRE, RODERICK, from Barra, emigrated on the brig Alexander of Greenock in June 1772, landed at Charlottetown, Prince Edward Island, on 25 June 1772. [PAPEI#2664/151]

MACINTYRE, RONALD, from South Uist, emigrated from Tobermory on the Emperor Alexander of Aberdeen, master Alexander Watt, to Sydney, Cape Breton, in July 1823, arrived there on 16 September 1823. [IJ:30.1.1824]

MCINTYRE, RORY, from Barra, emigrated on the brig Alexander of Greenock in June 1772, landed at Charlottetown, Prince Edward Island, on 25 June 1772. [PAPEI#2664/151]

MCISAAC, ANN, from Eilean Shona, Moidart, Inverness-shire, emigrated from Druimindarroch, Inverness-shire, aboard the Lucy bound for Prince Edward Island in July 1790. [SCA]

MCIVER, ALEXANDER, in Liberty County, Georgia, 1824. [NAS.RS.Inverness#248]

MCIVER, JOHN, in Alexandria, Virginia, 1798. [NAS.CS17.1.17/203]

MACKAY, AENEAS, a merchant in Boston, New England, and in Greenock, 1752. [NAS.RD4.178/1.553-556, 178/2.284]

MACKAY, ANGUS, born 1781, from Sutherland, emigrated from Cromarty on the Ossian of Leith, master John Hill, to Pictou, Nova Scotia, on 25 June 1821. [IJ:29.6.1821]

MCKAY, ARCHIBALD, in Bridge of Weir, to emigrate via Quebec to Upper Canada, 1820. [NAS.SC58.75.79]

MACKAY, JAMES, late of Montcoffer, died in Shannee Town on the Ohio, 18 September 1819. [S.4.155]

MACKAY, JOHN, a prisoner in Edinburgh Tolbooth, indented with James Mansfield a merchant in Edinburgh, for service in the American Plantations, and was sent to Glasgow for shipment in 1743. [NAS.HH11/22]

MCKAY, JOHN, from Bettyhill, Sutherland, Captain of the 27th Regiment of Foot, married Amelia Isabella, third daughter of Benjamin de Wolff, in Windsor, Nova Scotia, 1821. [S.5.249]

MCKAY, ROBERT, born 1751, with his family of eight, from Sutherland, emigrated from Cromarty on the Ossian of Leith, master John Hill, to Pictou, Nova Scotia, in June 1821. [IJ:29.6.1821]

MCKAY, WILLIAM, possibly from Caithness, then at Sugar
Loaf Mountain, Montgomery County, Maryland, by
1798. [NAS.CS177.1.16/45]

MCKEDDIE, DANIEL, born in 1730, an indentured servant
who absconded from Benjamin Duvall, Caroline
County, Virginia, on 3 June 1748. [MdGaZ#165]

MCKENZIE, Colonel ALEXANDER, Elizabeth City County,
Virginia, was admitted as a burgess and guilds-brother
of Ayr on 25 March 1729. [AyrBR]

MCKENZIE, ALEXANDER, with his wife Margaretha
Reitenbach, and their two children, from Charleston,
South Carolina, to Rotterdam, the Netherlands, by
October 1776. [Records of the Scots Church of
Rotterdam, Vol. I.60]

MCKENZIE, ANDREW, merchant in Virginia now in
Greenock, nephew of William McKenzie, merchant in
Edinburgh, 1789. [NAS.CS17.1.8/91]

MCKENZIE, ANDREW, late merchant in Virginia, granted
lands of Nether Carntyne on 6 August 1789.
[NAS.RGS.125/254] [NAS.CS17.1.8,129]

MCKENZIE, FARQUHAR, a planter in Jamaica, 1715.
[NAS.RD4.117.539]

MCKENZIE, JAMES, a merchant from Glasgow, died in
Annapolis, Maryland, on18 September 1748.
[MdGaz#178]

MCKENZIE, JOHN, formerly in Philadelphia, lost at sea,
inventory #1/52, 10 March 1809 Edinburgh

MACKENZIE, KENNETH, to Virginia as a chaplain on HMS
Severn, then a clergyman at St James, Lawn Creek,

near Williamsburg, Virginia, 1712. [NAS.NRAS.0040, bundle XIV]

MCKENZIE, PETER, a merchant from Forres, Morayshire, in America by 1802. [NAS.CS17.1.21/129]

MCKERRELL, Captain JOHN, in Norfolk, Virginia, husband of Frances Freeman, 1789. [NAS.CS17.1.8/338]

MCKEWEN, DONALD, born 1791, a laborer, with Allan McKewen born 1795, Angus McKewen born 1800, Mary McKewen born 1789, Isabella McKewen born 1798, and Effie McKewen born 1800, Kilfinichen, Mull, emigrated to Hudson Bay in 1812. [NAC.SP(C1), 294, 558-61]

MACKIE, ALEXANDER, a merchant in Virginia 7.5.1748. [NAS.B10.12.1.fo.178]

MACKIE, ANDREW, a merchant in Virginia, son of Andrew Mackie deacon of the dyers, 1766. [NAS.B10.15.7019]

MCKIE, GEORGE, possibly from Stranraer, a merchant in Baltimore 1800. [NAS.CS17.1.18/317; CS26/912, 48]

MACKIE, THOMAS, in Quebec, son of James Mackie a merchant in Findhorn, 1 August 1801. [NAS.RS.Elgin#567]

MCKINLAY, DONALD, born 1779, a laborer in Callendar, Perthshire, wife Margaret born 1782, children Margaret born 1811, and John born 1813, emigrated from Port Glasgow to St John, New Brunswick, on the Favorite of St John, master John Hyndman, 22 October 1815. [PANB:MS.RS23E/f9798]

MCKINNON, ALLAN, a carpenter from Barra, emigrated on the brig Alexander of Greenock in June 1772, landed at Charlottetown, Prince Edward Island, 25 June 1772. [PAPEI#2664/148]

MCKINNON, ANGUS, from Boisdale, from Boisdale, South Uist, emigrated on the brig Alexander of Greenock in June 1772, landed at Charlottetown, Prince Edward Island, 25 June 1772. [PAPEI#2664/151]

MCKINNON, ARCHIBALD, born 1772, his wife Marion M,cLean born 1776, and children Mary born 1810, and Alexander an infant, in Torinbeg, Kilfinichen, Mull, emigrated to Hudson Bay in 1812. [NAC.SP(C1), 294, 558-61]

MACKINNON, CHARLES, from Boisdale, South Uist, from Boisdale, South Uist, emigrated on the brig Alexander of Greenock in June 1772, landed at Charlottetown, Prince Edward Island, 25 June 1772. [PAPEI#2664/151]

MCKINNON, CHARLES WILLIAM, in St Augustine, Florida, 1776. [NAS.NRAS.0631.GDB.1776/1]

MCKINNON, JAMES, born around 1735, a convict indentured servant who absconded from Thomas Davis, Snowden's Iron Works, Maryland, on 18 July 1755. [MdGaz#533]

MCKINNON, LAUCHLAN, from Eigg, emigrated on the brig Alexander of Greenock in June 1772, landed at Charlottetown, Prince Edward Island, 25 June 1772. [PAPEI#2664/151]

MCKINNON, MARGARET, in Bellochyerran(?), to America on the Diamond of Glasgow, master Robert Arthur, in 1740. [NAS.SC54.48.14]

MCKINNON, NEIL, from Kinloch, shipwrecked on voyage to America 1775. [NAS.GD174.1303]

MCKINNON, NEIL, born 1782, with his wife Christina McLean, born 1787, and three sons and three daughters, in Torinbeg, Kilfinichen, Mull, emigrated to Hudson Bay in 1812, probably on the <u>Robert Taylor</u>. [NAC.SP(C1), 294, 558-62]

MCKINNON, NEIL, born 1767, with his wife Marjery McGilvra, born 1772, in Glen Baire, Kilfinichen, Mull, emigrated to Hudson Bay in 1812. [NAC.SP(C1), 294, 558-61]

MCKINNON, RONALD, Argyle, Nova Scotia, probate 8 June 1810, Prob.11/1512 PCC

MCKINNON, ..., daughter of Neil McKinnon from Rosall, shipwrecked on voyage to America 1775. [NAS.GD174.1303]

MACKINTOSH, Captain **ANGUS,** of Kellachy, died in Beaufort, Port Royal, South Carolina, in August 1779. [NAS.GD176.869]

MCLACHLAN, JAMES, a journeyman tailor, eldest son of John McLachlan a wright, emigrated to America 1756. [NAS.B10.15.6682]

MCLAINE, HECTOR, son of Hugh McLaine in Kilbhuheoin, Mull (?), shipwrecked on voyage to America, in New York 5.2.1776. [NAS.GD174.1303]

MCLAINE, JOHN, son of Lachlan McLaine in Correhinnach, shipwrecked on voyage to America, arrived there 1775. [NAS.GD174.1303]

MCLANE, ARCHIBALD, a factor in Virginia 1763. [BM.Add.#36218/199]

MCLAREN, ALEXANDER, born 1788, a laborer in Lochearnhead, Balquhiddder, wife Margaret born 1793, emigrated from Port Glasgow to St John, New Brunswick, on the <u>Favorite of St John</u>, master John Hyndman, 22 October 1815. [PANB:MS.RS23E/f9798]

MCLAREN, ARCHIBALD, born 1796, Callendar, Perthshire, emigrated from Port Glasgow to St John, New Brunswick, on the Favorite of St John, master John Hyndman, 22 October 1815. [PANB: MS.RS23E/f9798]

MCLAREN, JANET, born 1791, Callendar, Perthshire, emigrated from Port Glasgow to St John, New Brunswick, on the Favorite of St John, master John Hyndman, 22 October 1815. [PANB:MS.RS23E/f9798]

MCLAREN, ROBERT, born 1778, a laborer in Callendar, Perthshire, emigrated from Port Glasgow to St John, New Brunswick, on the Favorite of St John, master John Hyndman, 22 October 1815. [PANB:MS.RS23E/f9798]

MCLAUGHLIN, Mr, with 8 children, emigrated from Greenock on the George York, in 1810 to settle in Columbiana County, Ohio. [SHR#63/53]

MCLEA, ARCHIBALD, a merchant in St Johns, Newfoundland, later in New York, dead by 1820. [NAS.SC56.53.2/198]

MCLEAN, ALEXANDER, youngest son of Donald McLean in Achating, killed in Hudson Bay country, Spring 1816. [S.1.4][AJ#3605]

MCLEAN, ARCHIBALD, born 1787, a wright or joiner in Kilbrianan, Kilmore, Mull, emigrated to Hudson Bay in 1812. [NAC.SP(C1), 294, 558-61]

MCLEAN, DANIEL, died in Maryland before 1765. [NAS.GD174.142, 144]

MCLEAN, DONALD, formerly of Montgomery's Highlanders, an overseer for James Penman in East Florida, 1769. [NAS.NRAS.771, bundle 491]

MCLEAN, DONALD, born 1782, a wright, with his wife
Catherine Morrison born 1790, in Kilnienen, Kilmore,
Mull, emigrated to Hudson Bay in 1812. [NAC.SP(C1),
294, 558-61]

MCLEAN, DONALD, born 1790, a seaman, with his wife
Ann McLean, born 1788, Kilfinichen, Mull, emigrated
to Hudson Bay in 1812. [NAC.SP(C1), 294, 558-61]

MCLEAN, ELLEN, born around 1713, an indentured servant
who absconded from Joseph Tolson and Isaac
Winchester on Kent Island, Maryland, on 17 April
1754. [MdGaz#468]

MCLEAN, FRANCIS, Colonel of the 82nd Regiment, Halifax,
Nova Scotia, probate 9 March 1785, Prob.11/1127
PCC

MCLEAN, HECTOR, late of Kingerloch, died in Pictou, Nova
Scotia, 28.4.1810. [EA#4868]

MCLEAN, HECTOR, born 1784, with his mother Margaret
McInnis, his sister Mary McLean born 1796, Alexander
born 1788, a laborer, John McLean born 1790, and
Hugh McLean born 1794, in Cambus, Kilfinichen, Mull,
emigrated to Hudson Bay in 1812. [NAC.SP(C1), 294,
558-61]

MCLEAN, JOHN. Lieutenant of the 2nd Battalion, the Royal
Highland Emigrants Regiment, testament confirmed
1783, Edinburgh. [NAS]

MCLEAN, JOHN, born 1784, with his wife, born 1788, and
two children, born 1808 and 1810, in Kilbrianin,
Kilmore, Mull, emigrated to Hudson Bay in 1812.
[NAC.SP(C1), 294, 558-61]

MCLEAN, JOHN, a saddler in Halifax, Nova Scotia, 29 April
1823. [NAS.RD5.349.129; B22.4.22/239]

MCLEAN, LAUCHLAN, in Windsor, Nova Scotia, during 1785. [NAS.GD174/1382]

MCLEAN, LAUCHLAN, born 23 September 1754, son of Reverend Alexander McLean and Christian McLean in Kilninian, Mull, Lieutent Governor of Nova Scotia, died in Halifax. [F.4.115]

MCLEAN, MALCOLM, probably from Mull, arrived in Boston from Scotland 30 October 1773, settled in New Boston, sixty miles from Boston 20 December 1773. [NAS.GD174.1294]

MCLEAN, ..., with his wife, four children, and two servants, in Mull, emigrated to Hudson Bay in 1812. [NAC.SP(C1), 294, 558-61]

MCLELLAN, JANE, in Kirkcudbright, relict of William Meikle a merchant in Petersburg, Virginia, 1821. [NAS.CS17.1.40/306]

MACLELLAN, JOHN, from Kintail, emigrated from Tobermory on the Emperor Alexander of Aberdeen, master Alexander Watt, to Sydney, Cape Breton, in July 1823, arrived there on 16 September 1823. [IJ:30.1.1824]

MCLENNAN, RODERICK, from Kintail, emigrated from Tobermory on the Emperor Alexander of Aberdeen, master Alexander Watt, to Sydney, Cape Breton, in July 1823, arrived there on 16 September 1823. [IJ:30.1.1824]

MCLEOD, ALEXANDER, born 12 June 1774, son of Reverend Neil McLeod and Margaret McLean, minister of the Reformed Presbyterian congregation in New York. [F.4.113]

MCLEOD, ALEXANDER, born 1779, with his family of nine,

from Sutherland, emigrated from Cromarty on the
Ossian of Leith, master John Hill, to Pictou in June
1821. [IJ:29.6.1821]

MCLEOD, ARCHIBALD NORMAN, a merchant in Montreal,
1824. [NAS.CS17.1.44/68]

MCLEOD, DANIEL, of Kilmorie, a gentleman from Scotland,
via Philadelphia to Beckman township, Lake
Champlain, to view land he had brought to settled
Scottish families on, November 1773. [AJ#1362]; cf
Donald MacLeod, tacksman of Kilmorie, who
emigrated to America in 1773. [NAS.GD427.260]

MCLEOD, DONALD, tenant of Lord MacDonald in
Kendram, Skye, bound for America around 1802.
[NAS.GD221.4433.1]

MCLEOD, DONALD, tenant of Lord MacDonald in Maligar,
Skye, bound for America around 1802.
[NAS.GD221.4433.1]

MCLEOD, HUGH, born 1771, with his family of six, from
Sutherland, emigrated from Cromarty on the Ossian of
Leith, master John Hill, to Pictou in June 1821.
[IJ:29.6.1821]

MCLEOD, JAMES, son of Hugh McLeod of Geanies, a
storekeeper for Speirs and Company, in Maryland
1770-1772, in Virginia 1773-1775, thereafter a planter
in St Vincent 1776. [NLS#19297]

MCLEOD, JOHN, from Glenfinnan, son of Murdoch McLeod
of Harris, emigrated on the brig Alexander of
Greenock in June 1772, landed at Charlottetown,
Prince Edward Island, 25 June 1772.
[PAPEI#2664/145]

MCLEOD, MALCOLM, tenant of Lord MacDonald in
Maligar, Skye, bound for America around 1802.

[NAS.GD221.4433.1]

MCLEOD, NORMAN, a merchant in Boston, died 1767.
[NAS.NRAS.0623.T-MJ.377/c]

MCLEOD, RORY, tenant of Lord MacDonald in Kendram,
Skye, bound for America around 1802.
[NAS.GD221.4433.1]

MCMARTIN, JOHN, a thief, imprisoned in Stirling Tolbooth,
transported to America by William McAdam, burgess
of Stirling, and William Lang, a skipper in Greenock,
12 December 1754. [Stirling Vagabond Book]

MCMARTINE, NEILL, in Clackaig, Lergyside, Kintyre, to
America on the Diamond of Glasgow, master Robert
Arthur, in 1740. [NAS.SC54.48.14]

MCMARTINE, PATRICK, farmer in Murlaganmore,
Glenlochy, 'to emigrate to America' in 1786.
[NAS.GD112/11/1/4/49]

MCMASTER, ROBERT, absconded from the snow Edward,
master Abraham Weddett, in the Patuxent River,
Maryland, in August 1757. [MdGaz#653]

MCMASTER & INGLIS, merchants in New York, now in
Scotland, 1786. [NAS.CS17.1.5/362]

MCMILLAN, ANGUS, once a drover in Lochaber, then in
America, 1798. [NAS.CS17.1.17/203]

MCMILLAN, ARCHIBALD, a tidewaiter from Greenock,
then in America 1796. [NAS.CS17.1.15/399]

MCMILLAN, DONALD, a sailor, emigrated to Hudson Bay
on the Robert Taylor in 1812. [PAC.SP(C.1) 560-562]

MCMILLAN, DONALD, born 1793, a laborer in Port
Glasgow, emigrated from Port Glasgow to St John,

New Brunswick, on the Favorite of St John, master
John Hyndman, 22 October 1815.
[PANB:MS.RS23E/f9798]

MCMILLAN, JOHN, from Boisdale, South Uist, emigrated
on the brig Alexander of Greenock in June 1772,
landed at Charlottetown, Prince Edward Island, 25
June 1772. [PAPEl#2664/151]

MCMILLAN, JOHN, from Barra, emigrated on the brig
Alexander of Greenock in June 1772, landed at
Charlottetown, Prince Edward Island, 25 June 1772.
[PAPEl#2664/156]

MCMILLAN, WILLIAM, from Cambuslang, settled in
Dalhousie, Upper Canada, by 1822. [BPP.2.166]

MCMURDO, CHARLES, son of George McMurdo in Enrick,
Dumfries-shire, in Virginia, 1770, [NLS.Acc.7199, box
4/1]; in Virginia, 1789. [NAS.CS26/912, 10]

MCMURDO, GEORGE, a merchant in Virginia, 1751.
[NAS.CS96/2161/20]; son of George McMurdo in
Enrick, Dumfries-shire, in Virginia, 1770,
[NLS.Acc.7199, box 4/1]; in Virginia, later in Boreland
of Girthon, testament confirmed 1801 in Kirkcudbright.
[NAS.CC13.w4]

MCMURDO, JAMES, son of George McMurdo in Enrick,
Dumfries-shire, in Virginia, 1770, [NLS.Acc.7199, box
4/1];

MCMURDO, THOMAS, son of George McMurdo in Enrick,
Dumfries-shire, in Virginia, 1770, [NLS.Acc.7199, box
4/1]; in Virginia, 1789. [NAS.CS26/912.10]

MACNAB, ..., sons of Alexander MacNab of Inishewan,
Perthshire, emigrated to America in 1793.
[NLS.Acc.6945]

MCNAB, DAVID, born 1793, a laborer in Port Glasgow, emigrated from Port Glasgow to St John, New Brunswick, on the Favorite of St John, master John Hyndman, 22 October 1815. [PANB:MS.RS23E/f9798]

MCNAB, PATRICK, a herd and formerly a servant of Alexander Leach in Africk Milne, later in Stewarton, Ayrshire, guilty of fornication and ordered to be transported to Virginia in 1722. [Rothesay Kirk Session Records]

MCNAIR, JAMES, born 1 April 1794, son of Reverend James McNair and Agnes McNair in Slamannan, died in Mobile on 3 October 1823. [F#1.229]

MCNAIR, MALCOLM, released from Edinburgh Tolbooth for shipment to America via Glasgow on 24 January 1775. [ETR/NAS.HH11/28]

MCNAUGHTON, ALEXANDER, emigrated to America in 1738. [NLS.Acc.8168/box 2, 14]

MCNAUGHTON, DANIEL, a merchant in Montreal 1817, son of Donald McNaughton a merchant in Greenock and Flora Thomson, grandson of Alexander Thomson deputy tide surveyor of the Customs at Greenock. [NAS.SC53.56.1/ccxviii]

MCNAUGHTON, DUNCAN, emigrated to Hudson's Bay in 1812. [PCA.SP(C.1)560-562]

MCNAUGHTON, JOHN, born 1783, a laborer in Glasgow, with his wife Margaret born 1785, and children John born 1809, Janet born 1811, and William born 1813, emigrated from Port Glasgow to St John, New Brunswick, on the Favorite of St John, master John Hyndman, 22 October 1815. [PANB:MS.RS23E/f9798]

MCNAUGHTON, MALCOLM, born 1782, Strathfillan, Perthshire, emigrated from Port Glasgow to St John,

New Brunswick, on the Favorite of St John, master
John Hyndman, 22 October 1815.
[PANB:MS.RS23E/f9798]

MCNEIL, ANGUS, from Barra, emigrated on the brig
Alexander of Greenock in June 1772, landed at
Charlottetown, Prince Edward Island, 25 June 1772.
[PAPEI#2664/151]

MCNEIL, ARCHIBALD, from Colonsay, HM Consul for
Louisiana, died on his way from Canada to New York
1808. [EA#4607]; 1809. [NAS.CS17.1.29/104]

MCNEIL, GODFREY, from Argyll, arrived in Virginia on
board Captain McLarty's ship in December 1773.
[MdGaz#1478]

MCNEISH, GEORGE, sailor in New York, July 1752.
[NAS.CS16.1.89/17]

MCNERAN, MALCOLM, in Philadelphia 1818.
[NAS.SC56.53.2/95]

MCNICOLL, DONALD, Lieutenant of the 88th Regiment of
Foot 31 December 1774, Captain of the 84th {Royal
Highland Emigrants} Regiment 19 August 1780.
[NAS.RS10.Argyll.11.114: 12.29]

MCNIDER, MATTHEW, a merchant in Quebec, 1800.
[GA:T-ARD#13/1]

MCPHERSON, EVAN, and family, emigrated from
Greenock to New York on the Frances of New Orleans
in 1812, to settle in Highlandtown, Columbiana
County, Ohio. [SHR#63/53]

MCPHERSON, JAMES, alias Sutherland, alias James
Sommervill, a thief imprisoned in Lanark Tolbooth,
later in Edinburgh Tolbooth, released on condition of
leaving Great Britain and Ireland never to return in

1744. [NAS.HH11/22]

MCPHERSON, JAMES, a merchant in Edinburgh, later a Lieutenant in Montgomery's Highlanders in America June 1759. [NAS.CS16.1.105/78]

MCPHERSON, Captain, and his family, arrived in New York from Greenock on the George, Captain Boag, 18 July 1774. [SM.36.446]

MCPHERSON, Captain JOHN, of Philadelphia, Pennsylvania, late commander of HM man o' war Britannia in the West Indies, admitted as a burgess of Edinburgh by right of his father, 15 August 1764. [REB]

MCQUARLISH, ALEXANDER SUTHERLAND, born 1771, with his family of eight, from Sutherland, emigrated from Cromarty on the Ossian of Leith, master John Hill, to Pictou on 25 June 1821. [IJ:29.6.1821]

MCQUARLISH, DONALD SUTHERLAND, born 1771, with his family of nine, from Sutherland, emigrated from Cromarty on the Ossian of Leith, master John Hill, to Pictou on 25 June 1821. [IJ:29.6.1821]

MCQUEAN, DONALD, of Knockintavell, Jura, to America on the Diamond of Glasgow, Captain Robert McArthur, in 1740. [NAS.SC51.48.14]

MCQUEAN, DONALD, in Knockinlasell, to America on the Diamond of Glasgow, master Robert Arthur, in 1740. [NAS.SC54.48.14]

MCQUEEN, DAVID, in America 1723, husband of Euphame Shaw. [NAS.GD176.708]

MCQUEY, RICHARD, late a merchant in Virginia now in St Quivox, 1787. [NAS.NRAS.0623.T-MJ.122]

MACRA, ALEXANDER, from Kintail, emigrated from Tobermory on the Emperor Alexander of Aberdeen, master Alexander Watt, to Sydney, Cape Breton, in July 1823, arrived there on 16 September 1823. [IJ:30.1.1824]

MACRA, DUNCAN, from Kintail, emigrated from Tobermory on the Emperor Alexander of Aberdeen, master Alexander Watt, to Sydney, Cape Breton, in July 1823, arrived there on 16 September 1823. [IJ:30.1.1824]

MACRA, GEORGE, from Kintail, emigrated from Tobermory on the Emperor Alexander of Aberdeen, master Alexander Watt, to Sydney, Cape Breton, in July 1823, arrived there on 16 September 1823. [IJ:30.1.1824]

MACSWEEN, DONALD, tenant of Lord MacDonald in Upper Ollach, Skye, bound for America around 1802. [NAS.GD221.4433.1]

MCTAVISH, DONALD, in Lergnahsides(?), to America on the Diamond of Glasgow, master Robert Arthur, in 1740. [NAS.SC54.48.14]

MCTAVISH, DONALD, born in Stratherrick, a partner in the North West Company of Canada, drowned near the mouth of the River Columbia on the Pacific Coast, 22 May 1814. [AJ#3535]

MCTAVISH, SIMON, in Montreal, probate 17 October 1804, Prob.11/1416 PCC

MCVAERICH, GILBERT, tenant in Brainlain, Lergie, to America on the Diamond of Glasgow, master Robert Arthur, in 1740. [NAS.SC54.48.14]

MCVEAN, JAMES, tacksman of Inshdaive, Breadalbane, to emigrate to Nova Scotia in 1785. [NAS.GD112/16/4/1/2]

MCWILLIAM, JOHN, a merchant in Virginia and a debtor of the late John Johnstone, 1735, [see J.Johnstone's testament confirmed on 17 November 1735 in Dumfries]

MCWILLIAM, JANET, eldest daughter of William McWilliam, surgeon apothecary in Maryland, deceased, and William Clark, a merchant in Dumfries, subscribed to an ante-nuptial contract on 9 June 1764. [NAS.RH9.7.173]

MAIN, JAMES, a shoplifter, banished to America for life, at Aberdeen March 1768, [AJ#1054]; whipped through Aberdeen while awaiting shipment to the Plantations April 1768, [AJ#1056]; possibly transported on the George, master Peter Paterson, from Aberdeen to Virginia 25 May 1768. [AJ#1058]

MAIN, JAMES, son of George Main, a journeyman weaver in Leith, escaped from prison but recaptured, released from Edinburgh Tolbooth for transportation to the Plantations 27 December 1768. [NAS/HH11/28]

MAINS, WILLIAM, born 1787, a laborer in Port Glasgow, with his wife Margaret born 1790, and son William born 1812, emigrated from Port Glasgow to St John, New Brunswick, on the Favorite of St John, master John Hyndman, 22 October 1815. [PANB:MS.RS.23E/f9798]

MAIR, PETER, in North America 1808, only son of the late Alexander Mair feuar in Laurieston. [NAS.CS17.1.128/215]

MAITLAND, RICHARD, in Annapolis 1758. [NAS.NRAS.832.63.39]

MAITLAND, WILLIAM, of Valleyfield, 'many years a merchant in Virginia', died in Valleyfield 1812. [EA#5056]

MANBAY, GEORGE PEPPER, from Philadelphia, married Agnes Jolly the widow of George Vair, in the Canongate Kirk, Edinburgh, on 20 February 1777. [Canongate Marriage Register]

MANN, JOHN, born 1797, a laborer in Kenmore, Perthshire, emigrated from Port Glasgow to St John, New Brunswick, on the Favorite of St John, master John Hyndman, 22 October 1815. [PANB:MS,RS23E/f9798]

MANSON, WILLIAM, Orkney, a shipmaster in Philadelphia, 1773, a merchant in Augusta, Georgia, 10 February 1780. [NAS.NRAS.0627, box 9, bundle 2; box 18, bundle 12]

MARR, ANDREW, a merchant in Charleston, probate 27 September 1786, Prob.11/1146 PCC

MARR, ANN, prisoner in Edinburgh Tolbooth, released for transportation to America 20 April 1764. [NAS.HH#11/27]

MARSHALL, JAMES, Glasgow, emigrated 1747, a factor, died in Frederick County, Maryland, 1803. [AJ#2918]

MARSHALL, WILLIAM, a settler in Mississippi, 1794. [NAS.CS17.1.13,303]

MARSHALL, ZORABABEL, a former gaoler in Edinburgh, imprisoned in Edinburgh Tolbooth, released on condition of leaving Scotland, 11 March 1742. [NAS.HH11/21]

MARTIN, ALEXANDER, a shipbuilder from Port Glasgow, to America in April 1824. [NAS.SC53.56.4, cx]

MARTIN, ANDREW, son of John Martin of Craigmore, deceased, now in Virginia, 1789. [NAS.CS17.1.8/245]

MARTIN, JOHN, a merchant in Norfolk, Virginia, now in Kilquharity, Kirkcudbrightshire, 1785, 1794. [NAS.CS17.1.4/183; CS17.1.13,116]

MARTIN, MARTIN, tenant of Lord MacDonald in Balmeanach, Skye, bound for America around 1802. [NAS.GD221.4433.1]

MARTIN, WILLIAM, a thief, pardoned on condition of self-transportation to the Plantations, November 1750. [AJ#152]

MARTIN, WILLIAM, prisoner in Edinburgh Tolbooth, released for transportation to America 20 April 1764. [NAS.HH#11/27]

MARTINE, JAMES, "now in America", alleged father of Margaret born 5 March 1792. [Ayr OPR]

MATHESON, JOHN, late of Alladale, died in New York 24 October 1826. [AJ#4117]

MATHESON, NEIL, in Prince Edward Island, 1830. [NAS.GD90, sec.3, 34]

MEIKLE, THOMAS, a ships carpenter in New York, then in Leith Walk, Edinburgh, later in Greenock 1818. [NAS.CS17.1.38/595]

MEIN, THOMAS, in Vineyardhill, Georgetown, Potomac, Maryland, 1799. [NAS.CS17.1.18/377]

MELLISS, JOHN, born 1766, author of 'A Statistical Account of the United States', died in Philadelphia on 31 December 1822. [DPCA#1081] [EEC#17446]

MELVILLE, THOMAS, in Boston, admitted as a burgess of St Andrews, 13 September 1772. [St Andrews Burgess Roll]

MENZIES, JAMES, born 1795, a laborer in Glasgow,
emigrated from Port Glasgow to St John, New
Brunswick, on the Favorite of St John, master John
Hyndman, 22 October 1815. [PANB:MS.RS23E/f9798]

MERCER, Mrs JEAN, spouse to Mr David Alves in Quebec,
died in Edinburgh 7 January 1770. [AJ#1148]

MERRIWEATHER, Dr CHARLES, a physician in Edinburgh,
then in Virginia, 1795. [NAS.RS.Wigtown#455]

MERRYLEES, JAMES, son of James Merrylees at Upper
Bolton, in Savanna, Georgia, 1790/1795.
[NAS.CS17.1.9,8]

MIDDLETON, ALEXANDER, born in 1709, third son of
George Middleton and Janet Gordon, emigrated to
America, married Ann Todd in Boston, died 21 August
1750. [SP.VI.177]

MIDDLETON, PETER, a physician in New York 1772.
[NAS.RS27.202.203]

MILL, ALEXANDER, in New York, 1726. [NAS.RH9.1.221]

MILLAR, JAMES, born 1793, a laborer in Glasgow, with
wife Elizabeth born 1795, emigrated from Port
Glasgow to St John, New Brunswick, on the Favorite
of St John, master John Hyndman, 22 October 1815.
[PANB:MS.RS23E/f9798]

MILLER, DAVID, son of John Miller of Wellhouse, died in
Norfolk, Virginia, 14 October 1798. [AJ#2660]

MILLER, HUGH, late a merchant in Virginia, 1786, 1787,
1798 [NAS.CS17.1.5/20; CS17.1.6; CS17.1.17/350];
1792, [NAS.CS96.2026]

MILLER, JAMES, a merchant in Port Royal, Virginia, 1800.
[NAS.CS17.1.18/414]

MILLER, JEAN, widow of John Lawrie a miller in
Strathmiglo, Fife, then in America, 1809.
[NAS.CS17.1.28/442]

MILLER, JOHN, in Brighton, North America, 1820.
[NAS.CS17.1.39/357]

MILLER, JOHN, youngest son of James Miller of Hallhill,
now in Brighton, New York, 1820.
[NAS.CS17.1.39/199]

MILLER, ROBERT, a shipmaster in New York, 1795.
[NAS.CS17.1.14/99]

MILLER, ROBERT, late in Baltimore, deceased, and his
daughters Agnes and Harriet, 1819.
[NAS.CS17.1.39/27]

MILLER, THOMAS, carpenter in Virginia, 1789.
[NAS.CS17.1.8/284]

MILLER, WILLIAM, a chapman in Strathallan, now in
America, 1795. [NAS.CS17.1.14/247]

MILLER, WILLIAM, born 1775, with his family of five, from
Sutherland, emigrated from Cromarty on the Ossian of
Leith, master John Hill, to Pictou in June 1821.
[IJ:29.6.1821]

MILLIGAN, JAMES, a merchant in Philadelphia, 1770.
[NAS.RS23.XX.461]

MILLS, NATHAN, born in Boston, North America, 1751,
died in Edinburgh on 12 October 1824. [EEC#17646]

MILNE, JOHN, late a writer in Stonehaven, Kincardineshire,
then in America, 1798. [NAS.CS17.1.17/5]

MITCHELL, ALEXANDER, a surgeon in Ayr, settled in

Shepherdstown, Jefferson County, Virginia, husband of Eliza Kearsley, father of John Mitchell Kearsley born on 18 May 1793. [Ayr Old Parish Register]

MITCHELL, ELIZA, widow of David Morrison, sometime of New Orleans, 1813. [NAS.CS17.1.32/447]

MITCHELL, HENRY, a merchant in Fredericksburg, Virginia, 1781. [GM#IV/264]

MITCHELL, JAMES, in Maryland 1767, husband of Mary Stewart in Ayr, and father of John born 15 November 1767. [Ayr Old Parish Register]

MITCHELL, JAMES, in New York, 2 April 1823. [NAS.RD5.348.406]

MITCHELL, JOHN, a merchant in St Augustine, Florida, trading to the Mississippi, 31 October 1776. [NAS.NRAS.0159.C4]

MITCHELL, JOHN, a merchant in Virginia, 1782. [NAS.CS17.1.1/282]

MITCHELL, JOHN, late a chapman in Penningham, Galloway, then in America, 1783, 1799. [NAS.CS17.1.2.215; CS17.1.18/394]

MITCHELL, WILLIAM, a merchant in Demerara, died in Richmond, Virginia, 1805. [AJ#2992]

MITCHELL, WILLIAM, in Richmond, America, 1812. [NAS.RS54.PR130.55]

MITCHELL, WILLIAM, a merchant in Kingston, Canada, died there 24 September 1820. [AJ#3808][S.4.203]

MITCHELL, WILLIAM, in Virginia, 18 April 1826. [NAS.RD5.417.499]

MITCHELL, Lady, widow of Sir Andrew Mitchell, died in Halifax, Nova Scotia, 25 October 1825. [AJ#4070]

MITCHELSON, DAVID, in New York 1798, [NAS.RS.Argyll#1303]; late of New York, 4 December 1800 and 15 December 1800. [NAS.RS.Elgin#549/RS.Orkney#482]; died in Fife Place, Leith Walk, Edinburgh, on 24 October 1802. [EA#4033]

MOCHLINE, WILLIAM, from Rutherglen, Lanarkshire, a planter in Brunswick County, Virginia, by 1750. [NAS.RD2.168.10] [NAS.B64.1.7.151/7]

MOFFATT, JOHN, in Boston 1768. [NLS#CH3824]

MOFFATT, THOMAS, Customs Controller of the Port of New London 1768. [NLS#CH3824]

MOFFAT, Dr THOMAS, a Loyalist in Rhode Island, 1775. [PRO.T1.527.346-347]

MOIR, JOHN, released from Edinburgh Tolbooth for shipment to America via Glasgow 24 January 1775. [ETR/NAS.HH11/28]

MONACH, ANDREW, a merchant from Glasgow, then in America 1807. [NAS.CS17.1.26/16]

MONCRIEFF, ARCHIBALD, born 29 June 1751, son of Reverend Sir William Moncrieff and Katherine Wellwood in Blackford, Perthshire, a merchant in Baltimore, died 1803. [F.4.262]

MONCREIFF, ..., an apothecary from Edinburgh, later in America, 1796. [NAS.CS17.1.15/222]

MONRO, JAMES, sometime a messenger in Edinburgh, later in America, 1790. [NAS.CS17.1.9,69]

MONRO, JAMES, born 1771, son of James Monro the minister of Cromarty, settled in Pictou, Nova Scotia, in 1820, died there on 8 August 1843. [IC:13.9.1843]

MONRO, PETER, settled in Dalhousie, Upper Canada, by 1824. [BPP.2.166]

MONTGOMERIE, ALEXANDER, emigrated to America in 1738. [NLS.Acc.8168/box 2, 14]

MONTGOMERIE, JAMES, a merchant in New York, then in Haugh, parish of Urr, testament confirmed on 19 August 1801 in Dumfries. [NAS.CC5.18.251]

MONTGOMERY, HUGH, with four others, emigrated from Campbelltown to Prince Edward Island on the Edinburgh of Campbelltown, 27 July 1771. [NAS.SC54.2.106]

MONTGOMERY, THOMAS, formerly in Virginia, 1792/1794. [NAS.CS17.1.12,179; CS17.1.13/395]

MONTGOMERY, Mrs, wife of George Montgomery MD, died in Quebec 1818. [S#2/64]

MOOR, BENJAMIN, a carpenter in the Canongate, son of William Moor, a joiner in Pisealoqua, Rariton River, Middlesex County, New Jersey, 13 August 1762. [NAS.RS27.160.215]

MORGAN, ALEXANDER, a blacksmith in New York by 19 March 1819. [NAS.RS.Forfar#4/64]

MORRIS, JAMES PEMBERTON, born 1794 in Philadelphia, Pennsylvania, late in Lisbon, Portugal, landed at Bristol on 9 November 1813, a student, residing at Dr Gardner's, York Place, Edinburgh [ECA.SL115.2.2/71]

MORRISON, ALEXANDER, emigrated from Skye to America in August 1771. [Book of Dunvegan#II, bundle 26A/29]

MORRISON, ALEXANDER, born 1754, late a cooper in Aberdeen, died in Sham Cook, St Andrews, New Brunswick, 11 August 1814. [AJ#3543]

MORRISON, ALEXANDER, a tailor in Caithness, a robber imprisoned in Inverness Tolbooth then in Edinburgh Tolbooth, released for shipment to America for seven years, 4 December 1772. [NAS.HH11/28]

MORRISON, JAMES, in America, 1786. [NAS.CS17.1.5/45]

MORRISON, MARION, from South Uist, emigrated from Tobermory on the Emperor Alexander of Aberdeen, master Alexander Watt, to Sydney, Cape Breton, in July 1823, arrived there on 16 September 1823. [IJ:30.1.1824]

MORTIMER, EDWARD, born in Scotland 1768, a merchant, died in Pictou, Nova Scotia, 11 October 1819. [AJ#3750][S#3/149][EA#5841]

MUIR, ADAM, a merchant in Maryland, father of James Muir who matriculated at Glasgow University on 14 November 1746. [MAGU#35]

MUIR, JAMES, born in the Manse of Cumnock, Ayrshire, 12 April 1757, graduated MA from Glasgow University in 1776, minister of the Scots Presbyterian Church in Bermuda and principal of the Academy there from 1781 to 1788, minister of a Presbyterian church in Alexandria, Virginia, from 1789 to 1820, DD of Yale in 1819, died in Alexandria on 8 August 1820. [RGG#456]

MUIR, JOHN, a tailor in Annapolis, Maryland, about to return to Scotland in March 1748. [MdGaz#151]

MUIR, J.T., son of William Muir jr., merchant in Kilmarnock, died in Montreal 1817. [S.1.22]

MUIR, JOHN, Quebec, then in Dalserff House, testament confirmed on 15 October 1823 in Hamilton. [NAS.CC10.5.64]

MUIR, THOMAS, a wright in Edinburgh, banished to HM Plantations in America for life, released for transportation there by Peter Colquhoun 25 June 1773. [NAS.HH11/29]

MUIR, THOMAS, formerly in Maryland, died in Finnieston, Glasgow, in August 1779. [GM#IV.223]

MUIRHEAD, EBENEZER, a practioner of physick in Providence, Rhode Island, 1759. [NAS.RS23.XVII.7,11]

MUNDELL, THOMAS, younger son of Alexander Mundell, schoolmaster at Wallacehall Academy, and his wife Susanna Hepburn, a factor at Portobacco, Maryland, for Henderson, Gordon, Riddell and Company of Glasgow from 1784, later a merchant in Piscataway. [TDG#23/235]

MUNN, WILLIAM, born 1785, a laborer in Kenmore, emigrated from Port Glasgow to St John, New Brunswick, on the Favorite of St John, master John Hyndman, 22 October 1815. [PANB: MS.RS23E/f9798]

MUNRO, DAVID, a planter in Florida, 1790. [NAS.CS17.1.12,126]

MUNRO, HARRY, Captain of the 71st Regiment in Charleston, probate 23 June 1788, Prob.11/1167

MUNRO, JAMES, born in Cromarty 1 July 1772, son of Reverend James Munro and Mary Stark, a cabinet maker in Pictou, Nova Scotia. [F.7.5]

MUNRO, JOSEPH JOHN, from Virginia, sometime a student at Glasgow University, now in Edinburgh, 1788. [NAS.CS17.1.7/283]

MURRAY, Mr ALEXANDER, minister of Harr parish in Virginia in 1668, later around 1675 Dean of Killaley, Ireland. [NAS.AC7/4]

MURRAY, Dr ALEXANDER, graduated MA in 1746, an Episcopal priest and missionary in Reading, Pennsylvania, graduated DD at King's College, Aberdeen, on 17 February 1784. [KCA.103]

MURRAY, ALEXANDER, from Brechin, Angus, then in America 1796. [NAS.CS17.1.15/267]

MURRAY, JAMES, in Boston, husband of Margaret Mackay in Edinburgh, testament confirmed on 4 May 1786 in Edinburgh. [NAS]

MURRAY, JEAN, born 1796, with her family of one, from Sutherland, emigrated from Cromarty on the Ossian of Leith, master John Hill, to Pictou in June 1821. [IJ:29.6.1821]

MURRAY, JOHN, an Indian trader in Mobile, 1769, son of Andrew Murray in Arngask, Fife. [NAS.RD4.205.1]

MURRAY, JOHN, a merchant in New York, 1786. [NAS.CS17.1.5/350]

MURRAY, JOHN, Consul from the USA, died in Glasgow 1805. [AJ#2987]

MURRAY, MARGARET, a widow in Halifax, Nova Scotia, probate 6 September 1787, Prob.11/1157 PCC

MURRAY, MARGARET, born 1791, with her family of one, from Sutherland, emigrated from Cromarty on the

Ossian of Leith, master John Hill, to Pictou in June
1821. [IJ:29.6.1821]

MURRAY, ROBERT, a merchant in New York, 1786.
[NAS.CS17.1.5/350]

MURRAY, WILLIAM, a merchant in Petersburg, Virginia,
son of William Murray a merchant in Edinburgh, 1790.
[NAS.CS17.1.9,104]

MUTTER, JOHN, Richmond, Virginia, died in Naples 20
January 1819. [S.3.111]

MYLES, ALEXANDER, from Dundee, now in America,
1790. [NAS.CS17.1.9/28]

NAIRN, Lieutenant Colonel JOHN, died in Quebec in 1802.
[GA#1/75]

NAPIER, Sir JAMES, born 1711, former Inspector General
of HM Hospitals in North America, died in Wimpole
Street, London, January 1800. [AJ#2713][SM.61.907]

NEILSON, DAVID, in Canada 1 March 1816.
[NAS.RD5.310.291]

NEILSON, HUGH, a planter in Tanquair County, Virginia,
1785, 1799. [NAS.CS17.1.4/231; CS17.1.18/120]

NEILSON, JAMES, son of Gilbert Neilson a merchant in
Edinburgh, died in Baltimore, America, 4 July 1822.
[AJ#3841][S.5.239]

NEILSON, THOMAS, York County, Virginia, was admitted
as a burgess and guilds-brother of Ayr on 25 March
1729. [AyrBR]

NEILSON, WILLIAM, a merchant in Lewisburg, Virginia,
1785, 1799. [NAS.CS17.14/231; CS17.1.18/120]

NEWLANDS, JAMES, an indentured servant, shipped from Glasgow to Virginia in 1731, sought by Alexander Newlands, a skinner in Edinburgh, in April 1738. [NAS.RH15.5412] [VG#90]

NICOL, ALEXANDER, "under indenture to go to Georgia but having revolted was now absconding", 19 July 1738. [Elgin Kirk Session Records]

NICOLL, Reverend ANDREW, died at Richmond Bay, Prince Edward Island, 14 April 1820. [AJ#3787]

NICOLL, Dr JOHN, in New York, 1724. [PRO.SP54.14.28]; was admitted as a burgess and guilds-brother of Ayr on 10 April 1724. [AyrBR]

NICOLSON, DONALD, tenant of Lord MacDonald in Kendram, Skye, bound for America around 1802. [NAS.GD221.4433.1]

NICOLSON, JOHN, tenant of Lord MacDonald in Stenscholl, Skye, bound for America around 1802. [NAS.GD221.4433.1]

NICOLSON, JOHN, tenant of Lord MacDonald in Shulishadermor, Skye, bound for America around 1802. [NAS.GD221.4433.1]

NIMMO, WILLIAM, a merchant in Virginia, dead by 1816, his widow Marion Robertson in Linlithgow. [NAS.CS17.1.35/276]

NIVEN, DUNCAN, a merchant in Glasgow now in Virginia, 1786. [NAS.CS17.1.5/351]

NOBLE, ANGUS, and family, emigrated from Greenock to New York on the Frances of New Orleans in 1812, to settle in Highlandtown, Columbiana County, Ohio. [SHR#63/53]

NOBLE, JAMES, born in Mauchline, Ayrshire, merchant of the firm Noble and Arbuthnott in Norfolk, Virginia, died 30.5.1810. [EA#4869]

NORRIS, Dr HENRY, in Pennsylvania, graduated MD at King's College, Aberdeen, 7 December 1786. [KCA.136]

OGLETHORPE, JAMES, Trustee for the colony of Georgia, was admitted as a burgess and guildsbrother of Inverness, via his proxy Captain George Dunbar master of the Prince of Wales, 22 September 1735. [Inverness Burgess Roll]

OGILVIE, CHARLES, Banffshire, via London to Charleston in 1750, a merchant there, moved to London in 1761, died there in February 1788. [NAS.NRAS.0426.box 8, bundle 31] [AUL,MS2740:3/2, 3/19]

OGILVIE, GEORGE, Banffshire, settled in South Carolina before 1778. [NAS.NRAS.0426. box 31/34]

OGILVIE, JOHN ALEXANDER, in Georgia, 1788. [AUL.MS2740, 3/21]

OGILVIE, Dr WILLIAM, in Hanover County, Virginia, 1752. [AUL.MS2740, 2/5]

OGILVY, Colonel JOHN, died in Malden, America, on 28 September 1819. [S#3/149]

O'HEULY, ANGUS, from South Uist, emigrated from Tobermory on the Emperor Alexander of Aberdeen, master Alexander Watt, to Sydney, Cape Breton, in July 1823, arrived there on 16 September 1823. [IJ:30.1.1824]

O'HEULY, JOHN, from South Uist, emigrated from Tobermory on the Emperor Alexander of Aberdeen, master Alexander Watt, to Sydney, Cape Breton, in

July 1823, arrived there on 16 September 1823.
[IJ:30.1.1824]

O'HEULY, RANALD, from South Uist, emigrated from
Tobermory on the Emperor Alexander of Aberdeen,
master Alexander Watt, to Sydney, Cape Breton, in
July 1823, arrived there on 16 September 1823.
[IJ:30.1.1824]

OLIPHANT, JAMES, a jeweller and goldsmith from
Edinburgh, then in America, 1787.
[NAS.CS17.1.6/196]

OMAND, MARGARET, relict of Charles Gregory a skipper
in Prince George County, Virginia, brother of Harry
Omand, a skipper in Stromness, Orkney, 1792.
[NAS.RS.Orkney.288/289]

ORKNEY, Mrs, wife of James Orkney a jeweller in Quebec,
died in Montreal 1817. [S.1.37]

ORR, JOHN, a merchant in Virginia, 1786.
[NAS.CS17.1.5/45]

ORR, MARY, wife of James Fraser in Detroit then in
Aberdeen, testament confirmed on 17 June 1815.
[NAS.CC1.6.W967]

OSBURN, JAMES, mariner in Philadelphia, dead by 1740,
son of Reverend William Osburn in Fintray,
Aberdeenshire. [Process of Declarator of Marriage and
Legitimacy, Commissariot of Edinburgh, 1740, NAS]

PAGAN, ROBERT, late merchant in Falmouth, New
England, 1776. [NAS.SC58.61.13]

PAGAN, ROBERT, St Andrews, Charlotte County, New
Brunswick, 1822. [NAS.RS.869]

PARK, JOHN, a merchant in Virginia 1782.

[NAS.CS17.1.1/97]

PARK, ROBERT, a weaver from Glasgow, settled in Dalhousie township, Upper Canada, around 1821. [BPP.2.167]

PARKER, JACOB GODWIN, born 1783 in Accomack County, Virginia, later residing in Northampton County, Virginia, arrived at Gravesend on 9 June 1804, a student of physic, residing at Urquhart's Lodgings, 5 College Street, Edinburgh, in 1804. [ECA.SL115.2.2/34]

PARKER, JAMES, a merchant in Norfolk, Virginia, now in London 1794, later in Glasgow 1807. [LPL.ms25/271.PA16-31] [NAS.CS17.1.26/377]

PARKER, WILLIAM, a merchant in Montreal, co-owner of the Norval of Greenock, 1802. [NAS.CE60.11.7/49]

PATERSON, ALEXANDER, a merchant in USA, 1818. [NAS.SC58.7.49]

PATERSON, DAVID, born 1794, a laborer in Glasgow, emigrated from Port Glasgow to St John, New Brunswick, on the Favorite of St John, master John Hyndman, 22 October 1815. [PANB.MS.RS23E/f9798]

PATERSON, MATTHEW C., born 1794 in New York, arrived at Liverpool on 4 December 1815, a gentleman residing at 26 George Street, Edinburgh, by 16 December 1815. [ECA.SL115.2.2/74]

PATERSON, SIMON, a merchant in Georgia 1802. [NAS.CS17.1.21/287]

PATERSON, WILLIAM, from Aberdeen, a seaman on the Dolphin of Philadelphia, Captain O'Bryen, was captured and taken prisoner to Algiers in July 1785. He was still in captivity in July 1790. [AJ#2230]

PATTERSON, THOMAS, a ropemaker in Leith, then in Baltimore, Maryland, 1780, 1810. [NAS.RS27.250.260; CS17.1.30/87]

PATON, ROBERT, merchant in Fredericksburg, Virginia, 1789. [NAS.CS17.1.8/198]

PATRICK, ROBERT, a merchant in St George, Bermuda, probate 20 June 1811, Prob.11/1523 PCC

PATTEN, THOMAS, a merchant in St John's, Newfoundland, co-owner of the Irvine of Greenock, 1806. [NAS.CE60.11.8/10]

PAUL, JAMES, a brewer in New York, heir portioner to John Henderson a brewer in Linlithgow. 1821. [NAS.B48/18/69]

PEACOCK, HUGH, a tailor from Newton Stewart, now in America, husband of Hannah Nairne, testament confirmed in 1785 Edinburgh. [NAS]

PEDINE, JAMES, natural son of James Pedine of Burnshiel, Ayrshire, settled in Virginia by 1778. [NAS.CS16.1.173/128]

PENMAN, JAMES, formerly a clerk to Peter Taylor, an army contractor in Germany, an estate manager in East Florida 1766, arrived in St Augustine, East Florida, 1772. [NAS.NRAS.771: bundles 295/491]; a merchant in Charleston, probate 26 November 1789, Prob.11/1185 PCC

PERCIVAL, JOHN, born 1785, a laborer in Port Glasgow, emigrated from Port Glasgow to St John, New Brunswick, on the Favorite of St John, master John Hyndman 22 October 1815. [PANB:MS.RS23E/f9798]

PERRIE, ALEXANDER, an indentured servant who

absconded from D. Dulany in Annapolis, Maryland, in December 1745. [MdGaz#55]

PETER, ALEXANDER, a merchant in Virginia, 1787. [NAS.CS17.1.6,358]

PETER, WALTER, in Virginia, 1763. [NAS.GD180.348]; a merchant in Virginia, 1787. [NAS.CS17.1.6/198]

PETERKIN, L., late of Glasgow, died in New York on 12 August 1803. [EEC#14321]

PETTIGREW, JAMES, in Virginia, dead by 1788. [NAS.CS17.1.7,165]

PHILIPSHILL, CHARLES, in Warwick, Cecil County, Maryland, 1789. [NAS.CS17.1.8/200]

PIRIE, ADAM, a housebreaker, imprisoned in Haddington Tolbooth and later in Edinburgh Tolbooth, released for shipment from Leith to Maryland on the Mally of Glasgow, Captain Peacock, on 20 September 1769. [NAS.HH11/28]

POLLOCK, ALLAN, deceased, Virginia, 1820. [NAS.CS17.1.39/406]

POLLOCK, ALLAN, yr., merchant in Richmond, Virginia, 1822. [NAS.CS17.1.42/319]

POLLOCK, JOHN, merchant on the James River, Virginia, eldest son of John Pollock portioner of Overton of Auchenbothieblair, Lochwinnoch, Renfrewshire, 1800, 1801. [NAS.CS17.1.19/123; CS17.1.9/112; CS18.708.4]

POLLOCK, JOHN, of Logie Green W.S., died in Yanceyville, Virginia, 26.4.1817. [S.1.21]

POLLOCK, ROBERT, a merchant in Petersburg, Virginia,

inventory dated 16 June1813 in Edinburgh
[NAS.SC70.1.8.307]

POLLOCK, ROBERT, a merchant in Petersburg, Virginia,
son of Allan Pollock and Janet Morris in Glasgow,
1817. [NAS.CS17.1.37/89]

POLLOCK, ROBERT, a merchant in Richmond, Virginia,
1822. [NAS.CS17.1.42/319]

PORTEOUS, JOHN, a merchant in New York, 1786.
[NAS.CS17.1.5/310]

PORTER, JOHN, a Scots-American student at Glasgow
University 1703. [MUG#179]

POTTIE, WILLIAM, in Louisa County, Virginia, 1801.
[NAS.CS17.1.9/335]

POWER, N. surgeon, formerly in Newfoundland, died in
Miramachi, New Brunswick, on 26 October 1817.
[S.1.47]

PRINGLE, BEATRIX, in Canada, 17 April 1830.
[NAS.RD5.414.55]

PROCTOR, Reverend WILLIAM, born in Banff or Elgin,
educated at Aberdeen College, died in Nottoway
parish, Virginia, 1761. [AJ#741]

PROSIT, CHARLES, possibly from Dundee, settled in New
Orleans, Louisiana, by 1805. [NAS.CS17.1.24/147]

PROVAN, MATTHEW, in Maryland, 1 October 1726 and 17
November 1726. [NAS.RS10.Dunbarton.5#384/405]

PROVAN, ROBERT, a thief imprisoned in Glasgow
Tolbooth and later in Edinburgh Tolbooth, released for
shipment to America via Glasgow on 15 March 1773.
[NAS.HH11/28]

PURVES, JOHN HOME, of Purves, HM Consul for Florida, died in Pensacola 30 September 1827. [AJ#4172]

RAE, GEORGE, late in Virginia, then in Dumfries 1793. [NAS.CS17.1.12,378]

RAGG, ANNA, daughter of Andrew Ragg in Maryland, married Andrew Bissett, Customs Controller in Montrose, in Aberdeen on 30 April 1800. [AJ#2730]

RALSTON, ALEXANDER, a carrier, sometime in St Ninian's, Stirling, settled in North America by 1805. [NAS.CS17.1.24/245]

RALSTON, PETER, a tanner, sometime in St Ninian's, Stirling, settled in North America by 1806. [NAS.CS17.1.25/37]

RAMSAY, JAMES, formerly in New Orleans then in Alloa, 1818. [NAS.CS17.1.38/338]

RAMSAY, JOHN, a merchant from Alloa, Clackmannanshire, then in North America, 1796. [NAS.CS17.1.15/403]

RAMSAY, ROBERT, from Maybole, Ayrshire, a wright in Baltimore 1819. [NAS.CS17.1.38/528]

RAMSAY, WILLIAM, a merchant in Virginia, 1782. [NAS.CS17.1.1.411]

RAMSAY,............, a weaver from Glasgow, settled in North Sherbrook township, Upper Canada, around 1821. [BPP.2.167]

RANALDSON, JAMES, in Philadelphia, 10 March 1794. [NAS.RD.338.114]

RANKIN, ALAN, in Bridge of Weir, to emigrate via Quebec

to Upper Canada, 1820. [NAS.SC58.75.79]

RAVENSCROFT, Dr JOHN, of Cairnsmuir, late in Maycox, Virginia, 1775. [NAS.RS23.XXI.327]; was granted lands of Bardrochwood on 23 February 1776. [NAS.RGS.116/112]

REID, GEORGE, a surgeon, St John, New Brunswick, probate 6 April 1784, Prob.11/1116 PCC

REID, ISABELLA, sister of late Robert Reid in Savanna, Georgia, 1798. [NAS.CS17.1.17/11]

REID, JOHN, a bookseller in New York, 1789. [NAS.CS17.1.8/45]

REID, JOHN, a merchant in Virginia, son of the deceased James Reid in Dumfries, died in London on 13 November 1791. [GCr#37]

REID, R., deceased, late of Savanna, Georgia, pre1798. [NAS.CS17.1.17/11]

REID, THOMAS, a merchant in Virginia, died before 1801. [NAS.CS17.1.9/234]

RENNIE, DAVID, a merchant in St John's, Newfoundland, co-owner of the Diana of Greenock, the Brothers of Greenock, 1801, and of the Jessie of Greenock, 1801. [NAS.CE60.11.5/28; 7/12/15]

RICHARDSON, JAMES, late a merchant in Glasgow, died in New York 2 September 1799. [AJ#2703]

RICHARDSON, ROBERT, at Oxford Ironworks, Lynchburg, Virginia, July 1816. [NAS.CS17.1.35/636]

RIDDELL, ALEXANDER, from Virginia, now in Dumfries, 1799. [NAS.CS17.1.18/189]

RIDDELL, HENRY, partner of John Glassford in Maryland before 1776, resident in Pitcataway on the Potomac River, returned to Britain 1778. [PRO.AO12.9.fo.19]

RIDDOCH, ALEXANDER, a merchant in Virginia 1798, son of William Riddoch of Corbieston. [NAS.CS17.1.17/51];brother of the late William Riddick of Corbieston, Captain of the 22nd Regiment of Foot, 1799, [NAS.CS26.906.2]; in Dumfries 1800. [NAS.CS17.1.19/23]

RITCHIE, JAMES, in Maryland, 1804. [NAS.CS17.1.23/154]

ROBB, JAMES, son of William Robb a merchant in Glasgow, factor for Patrick Mitchell in Port Royal, Virginia, 1753-1756. [GA.T-MJ]

ROBERTS, MERCER, son of Edward Roberts a saddler in Willimsburg, Virginia, apprenticed to Baillie Blinshall, a saddler in Edinburgh, for 7 years, on 15 October 1778. [ERA]

ROBERTSON, DAVID DUNCAN, son of Samuel Robertson in Ednam, died in Savannah, Georgia, 1817. [S.1.31]

ROBERTSON, GEORGE, a tanner from Glasgow, then in Virginia, 1794. [NAS.CS17.1.13,10]

ROBERTSON, JAMES, born 1729, an indentured servant who absconded from Anthony Smith in Prince George's County, Maryland, on 4 February 1754. [MdGaz#458]

ROBERTSON, JAMES, of the Hudson Bay Company, 7 October 1807. [NAS.RS.Orkney#730]

ROBERTSON, JAMES, in New York 20.11.1826. [NAS.RS.Dysart#2/112]

ROBERTSON, JAMES, son of the late Robert Robertson in

Caroline County, Drysdale parish, Virginia, sought in Edinburgh in December 1771. [EA:28.12.1771]

ROBERTSON, JAMES, of Struan, Prince Edward Island, then in Edinburgh, 1821. [NAS.CS17.1.40/236]

ROBERTSON, JOHN, sentenced in 1776 to transportation to the colonies. [PRO.SP54.46.186]

ROBERTSON, JOHN, son of John Robertson a cooper in Glasgow, a seaman on the Dolphin of Philadelphia, Captain O'Bryen, was captured and taken to Algiers in July 1785. He was still in captivity in July 1790. [AJ#2230]

ROBERTSON, Dr JOHN STARK, in New York, 8 December 1797. [NAS.SC20.33.13]

ROBERTSON, JOHN, fourth son of Thomas Robertson, sometime a journeyman baker in Edinburgh later in Baltimore or Philadelphia, 1802. [NAS.CS17.1.21/353]

ROBERTSON, JOHN, in Sussex County, Virginia, 1796, 1808, eldest son of John Robertson a thread manufacturer in Paisley, Renfrewshire. [NAS.CS17.1.15/399; CS17.1.27/35]

ROBERTSON, RICHARD, a sailor in Dundee, a housebreaker, released from Edinburgh Tolbooth for shipment to America by Patrick Colquhoun, on 17 March 1773. [NAS.HH11/29]

ROBERTSON, THOMAS, son of the late Robert Robertson in Caroline County, Drysdale parish, Virginia, sought in Edinburgh in December 1771. [EA:28.12.1771]

ROBERTSON, WILLIAM, in New York, by 1750. [NAS.RD4.176/1.448]

ROBERTSON, WILLIAM, a merchant in Greenock, via

Liverpool to America, 1801. [NAS.CS17.1.20/467]

ROBERTSON, WILLIAM, from Renfrew, a merchant in
Yarmouth, Shelburne, Nova Scotia, 1803, 1809.
[NAS.SC58.61.21; CS17.1.28/320]

ROBERTSON, WILLIAM, in Petersburg, USA, 1816.
[NAS.RS.Forfar.2.226]

ROBINSON, SAMUEL, born 1774 in Philadelphia, late in
Petersburg, landed at Hull on 27 October 1819, a
chemist, residing in Richmond Place, Edinburgh, by
November 1819. [ECA.SL115.2.2/90]

ROGER, RICHARD, a writer from Dundee, and his family,
drowned in the wreck of the brig Margaret near Sable
Island 29 October 1821. [AJ#3841]

ROGERSON, JAMES, merchant in St John's,
Newfoundland, co-owner of the Trepalsay of
Greenock, 1805, and of the Hope of Greenock, 1806.
[NAS.CE60.11.8/15/14]

ROME, THOMAS, of Clouden, a merchant in Antigua, 1715.
[NAS.RD2.104.657]

RONALDSON, JAMES, in Philadelphia, 1794, and in 1828.
[NAS.RD5.338.114; RD5.367.338]

RORIESON, ROBERT, of Ardoch, Lieutenant of the 37th
Regiment in America, 1778. [NAS.CS16.1.173/34]

ROSE, JAMES, an excise officer in Muthill, Perthshire,
banished to America for forgery, 4 February 1757.
[NAS.HH11]

ROSE, JOHN, from Forres, Morayshire, then in Essex,
America, 1747. [NAS.RH1.2.861]

ROSE, JOHN, born 1803, Ensign of the 70th Regiment of

Foot, son of Major Rose of the 6th Royal Veteran Battalion, died in Amherstburg, Upper Canada, 21 January 1827. [AJ#4135]

ROSE, JOHN, late of Nigg, Ross-shire, died in Lycoming, Pennsylvania, 1812. [AJ#3390][EA#5111]

ROSE, ROBERT, son of John Rose of Ormly, died in Richmond, Virginia, 1805. [AJ#2992]

ROSIE, EDWARD JAMES, in Norfolk, Virginia, grandson of Edward Rosie of Sucquoy, Sandwick, South Ronaldsay, Orkney Islands, 23 April 1802. [NAS.RS.Orkney.511]

ROSS, CHR., born 1801, with his family of one, from Sutherland, emigrated from Cromarty on the Ossian of Leith, master John Hill, to Pictou in June 1821. [IJ:29.6.1821]

ROSS, DAVID, a merchant from Thurso, Caithness, then in a Hudson Bay Company Fort by 1753. [NLS.CH3819]

ROSS, DAVID, a merchant in Baton Rouge, West Florida, 1787. [NAS.CS17.1.6/15]

ROSS, DAVID, a merchant in Petersburg, Virginia, 1789. [NAS.CS17.1.8,232]

ROSS, DAVID, a tenant in Manorleys, Portmoak, Kinross, then in America 1818. [NAS.CS17.1.38/363]

ROSS, DONALD, born 1802, with his family of one, from Sutherland, emigrated from Cromarty on the Ossian of Leith, master John Hill, to Pictou in June 1821. [IJ:29.6.1821]

ROSS, EDWARD JOHNSTON, portioner of Sonquay in South Ronaldsay, now in Virginia, 1820. [NAS.CS17.1.39/253]

ROSS, ELIZABETH, in Elizabeth City, North Carolina, probate 28 November 1768, Prob.11/944

ROSS, GEORGE, a merchant in Shelburne, Nova Scotia, probate 2 June 1818, Prob.11/1760 PCC

ROSS, HECTOR, a merchant in Colchester, Virginia, 1786. [NAS.CS17.1.15/134]

ROSS, HUGH, a merchant planter in Georgia, settled in Scotland 1815, bought Knockbrake in Ross-shire. [NAS.CS97, box 106]

ROSS, JAMES, a witness in Pensacola to John Murray's deed, 18 February 1769. [NAS.RD4.205.1]

ROSS, JAMES, from Shetland, a shipmaster in New Providence, 1819. [NAS.CS17.1.38/359]

ROSS, JOHN, born 1730, a Highland indentured servant, absconded from Fredericksburg on 20 July 746. [MdGaz#76]

ROSS, JOHN, a merchant from Loch Broom then in America, now in Edinburgh, 1782. [NAS.CS17.1.1.80]

ROSS, JOHN, a merchant, from Greenock to Philadelphia on the Charlotte of Philadelphia, master Peter Bell, in February 1796. [NAS.E504.15.71]

ROSS, JOHN, tenant of Lord MacDonald in Kendram, Skye, bound for America around 1802. [NAS.GD221.4433.1]

ROSS, MALCOLM, late in Philadelphia, 1786. [NAS.CS17.1.5/237]

ROUGHEAD, JAMES, a merchant in Port Royal, Jamaica, eldest son of Thomas Roughead of Whitsomehill, Berwickshire, husband of Jean Coupar, 1715.

[NAS.RD3.144.151; RD4.117.295]

ROWAND, JOHN, from Paisley, Renfrewshire, a merchant in Virginia, 1787, 1801. [NAS.CS17.1.6/288; CS17.1.9/383]

ROWAND, ROBERT, son of Thomas Rowand in Dumfries, a thief imprisoned in Dumfries, transported from Dumfries to Virginia on the Kirkconnell of Dumfries in January 1715. [DGA.GF4.19A.10]

ROWAND, THOMAS, in Lancaster, Virginia, deceased by 1787, and his children Thomas, Joseph. and Juda. [NAS.CS17.1.6,288; 7/97]

ROXBURGH, JOHN, released from Edinburgh Tolbooth for shipment to America via Glasgow on 24 January 1775. [NAS.HH11/28]

RULES, ROBERT, writer in Edinburgh, now in New York, 1820.[NAS.CS17.1.39/579]

RUSSELL, ALEXANDER, an auctioneer and builder in Glasgow, a bankrupt in 1826 who emigrated to America. [NAS.CS238/C18/37]

RUSSELL, JOHN, late in Montreal, 1801. [NAS.RS.Glasgow#4136]

RUSSELL, JOHN, in Philadelphia, 27 February 1827. [NAS.RD5.342.477]

RUSSELL, ROBERT, a wright in Edinburgh later in New York, 1820. [NAS.CS17.1.39]

RUSSELL, SAMUEL, in Marblehead, Essex County, Massachusetts, probate 1 September 1722. [NAS.GD155.465]

RUSSELL, WILLIAM, born in Cumnock, Ayrshire, 1764, a

merchant, died in Charleston, South Carolina, 16 January 1815. [AJ#3528]

RUTHERFORD, Mrs C., wife of Walter Rutherford, died in New York 1801. [AJ#2801]

RUTHERFORD, WALTER, of New Edgerston, died in New York 1803. [AJ#2933]

RUTHVEN, THOMAS, released from Edinburgh Tolbooth for shipment to America via Glasgow on 24 January 1775. [NAS.HH11/28]

SABISTON, ALEXANDER, Hudson Bay Company, testament confirmed on 31 October 1807 Orkney. [NAS.CC17.3.1.7]

SCLATER, DAVID, in Franklin County, North Carolina, 1824. [NAS.CS17.1.44/94]

SCOBIE, ANDREW, in Bridge of Weir, to emigrate via Quebec to Upper Canada, 1820. [NAS.SC58.75.79]

SCOTT, ALEXANDER, Lancaster County, Pennsylvania, probate 16 March 1824, Prob.11/1683 PCC

SCOTT, ANDREW, in Maryland 6 August 1739. [BM.Sloane MS#4056/110]

SCOTT, ANDREW, born in Paisley, died in Portland, America, in September 1818. [S#3/95]

SCOTT, JOHN, a minister in Prince William County, Virginia, died at General Wood's near Winchester 22 July 1784. [AJ#1920]

SCOTT, JOHN, a merchant in Charleston, probate 30 August 1791, Prob.11/1208 PCC

SCOTT, JOHN, born 1751, a merchant in St John's,

Newfoundland, died in Edinburgh, on 17 March 1829.
[East Preston Street cemetery, Edinburgh]

SCOTT, JOHN, of the Hudson Bay Company, then in
Stromness, Orkney Islands, 1834.
[NAS.RS.Orkney#167]

SCOTT, MICHAEL, born ca1783 in Port Dundas, settled in
Quebec. [NAS.NRAS.0390.TD217.14]

SCOTT, ROBERT, a merchant in Virginia, 1794.
[NAS.CS17.1.13,294]

SCOTT, THOMAS, paymaster of the 7th Regiment, brother
of Sir Walter Scott, died in Quebec 14.2.1823.
[DPCA#1079]

SCOTT, WILLIAM, of Wooll, died in Quebec 12 March
1820. [AJ#3764]

SCOTT, Mrs, relict of Reverend John Scott, and daughter of
Professor Gordon of King's College, Aberdeen, died in
Gordon's Vale, Virginia, 15 July 1802. [AJ#2854]

SELKIRK, JOHN, son of Robert Selkirk late a merchant in
Boston, apprenticed to William Jamieson, a mason in
Edinburgh, for 6 years, on 20 November 1788. [ERA]

SHAW, Lieutenant ALEXANDER, adjutant of the 60th Royal
American Regiment of Foot, 6 October 1761.
[NAS.GD103.2.412]

SHAW, ALEXANDER, bookseller, late of Turnbull and
Shaw in Virginia, now in Kingston, Jamaica, 1789.
[NAS.CS17.1.8/90]

SHAW, DAVID, born around 1718, a tailor, broke bail in
Cambridge, Dorchester County, Maryland, on 9 April
1748. [MdGaz#161]

SHAW, MARGARET, spouse of Dr James Flint a physician in Petersburg, Virginia, 1798. [NAS.CS17.1.17/121]

SHAW, THOMAS, born 1794, a laborer in Dunbarton, emigrated from Port Glasgow to St John, New Brunswick, on the Favorite of St John, master John Hyndman on 22 October 1815. [PANB:MS.RS23E/f9798]

SHAW, WILLIAM, Quebec, was admitted as a burgess and guildsbrother of Ayr on 7 February 1784. [AyrBR]

SHEDDAN, JOHN, a merchant in Virginia 1783. [NAS.CS17.1.2.248]

SHEDDEN, WILLIAM, late in Beith, now in America 1788. [NAS.CS17.1.7/265]

SHEDDEN, WILLIAM, of Roughwood, a merchant in New York, died there 13 November 1798. [AJ#2661][EWJ.2.54]

SHEPHERD, Dr WILLIAM, Orange County, Virginia, 1806. [GA.T-ARD#13/1]

SHIELS, JOHN, alias WILSON, guilty of stealing sheep, released from Edinburgh Tolbooth for transportation from Leith to Maryland on the Mally of Glasgow, Captain Peacock, on 20 September 1769. [NAS.HH11/28]

SHORT, JOHN, in Virginia, father of James, 1784, 1797. [NAS.CS17.1.3/353;16/14]

SIBBALD, GEORGE, a merchant in St Mary's, Georgia, by 1807. [NAS.CS17.1.26/474]

SIBBALD, JOHN, a merchant in Philadelphia in 1772, son of David Sibbald, a shipmaster in Kirkcaldy, Fife, and his wife Janet Hoggan. [NAS.B41.7.8/187]

SILLIMAN, BENJAMIN, born 1779 in Trumbull,
Connecticut, a gentleman from Newhaven,
Connecticut, arrived at Liverpool on 3 May 1805,
residing at 3 Fyfe Street, Edinburgh, by November
1805. [ECA.SL115.2.2/42]

SIMPSON, JOHN, a merchant, died in Nassau, New
Providence, on 4 January 1790. [AJ#2204]

SINCLAIR, FLORY, emigrated from Campbelltown to Cape
Fear, North Carolina, on the Edinburgh of
Campbelltown, on 27 July 1771. [NAS.SC54.2.106]

SINCLAIR, JAMES, in Nova Scotia, son of Isabel Lamont
sister of Lauchlan Lamont of Achagoyle, 17 January
1782. [NAS.CS17.1.1/10]

SINCLAIR, JAMES, at York Fort, Hudson Bay, 2 August
1797. [NAS.RS.Orkney#407]

SINCLAIR, JOHN, late in Carsebuie, now a planter in
Faquier County, Virginia, grandson of John Sinclair, a
merchant in Newton Stewart, Wigtonshire, 1801.
[NAS.RS.Wigton#617]

SKENE, ALEXANDER, a merchant in Norfolk, Virginia,
1730, brother of George Skene of that Ilk.
[NAS.GD237/20/8/32]

SKENE, WILLIAM, a surgeon in Annapolis, Nova Scotia,
probate 11 March 1773, prob.11/986 PCC

SLATER, JAMES, of the Hudson Bay Company, 6 July
1810. [NAS.RS.Orkney#805]

SMILLIE, DAVID, a shipmaster in Halifax, Nova Scotia, then
in Paisley, Renfrewshire, 1815. [NAS.SC58.5.227]

SMITH, ALEXANDER, in Runachan, to America on the

Diamond of Glasgow, master Robert Arthur, in 1740. [NAS.SC54.48.14]

SMITH, ANDREW, born 1790, a surgeon, late of Montreal, died in Smithfield, 21 April 1824. [Riccarton, Ayrshire, gravestone]

SMITH, ARCHIBALD, emigrated from Campbelltown to Cape Fear, North Carolina, on the Edinburgh of Campbelltown, 27 July 1771. [NAS.SC54.2.106]

SMITH, D.A., in North America, 1828. [NAS.RD5.361.159]

SMITH, DUNCAN, in Runcahan, to America on the Diamond of Glasgow, master Robert Arthur, in 1740. [NAS.SC54.48.14]

SMITH, GEORGE, from Portsoy, Banffshire, a seaman on the Dolphin of Philadelphia, Captain O'Bryen, was captured and taken to Algiers in July 1785. He was still in captivity in July 1790. [AJ#2230]

SMITH, JAMES, born 1714, schoolmaster in Urquhart or Glen Moriston, emigrated via Mull to New York on the Moore of Greenock, Captain McLarty, in July 1774. [AJ#1387]

SMITH, JAMES, a weaver from Glasgow, settled in North Sherbrook township, Upper Canada, around 1821. [BPP.2.167]

SMITH, JAMES, second son of John Smith, Largo, Fife, died in Savannah, Georgia, 25 October 1817. [S#2/52]

SMITH, MALCOLM, in Lergyside, Kintyre, to America on the Diamond of Glasgow, master Robert Arthur, in 1740. [NAS.SC54.48.14]

SMITH, Colonel NICOLAS, Elizabeth City County, Virginia, was admitted as a burgess and guilds-brother of Ayr on 25 March 1729. [ABR]

SMITH, THOMAS, in Whiteriggs, Dumfries, a horse thief, transported to America in 1744. [DGA.GF4.21.09]

SMITH, WILLIAM, in Cambridge, North America, 1784. [NAS.CS17.1.3/140]

SMITH, WILLIAM, in Halifax, Nova Scotia, co-owner of the Lord Macartney of Greenock, William of Greenock, & the Cato of Greenock 1798, the Liberty of Greenock, the Sophy of Greenock, 1804, the Lady Parker of Greenock, 1804, the Caledonian of Greenock, 1804, the Lilly of Greenock 1804, and the Thomas of Greenock, 1805. [NAS.CE60.11.5/64/187; 6/17; 8/58/64/5/9/10]

SNODGRASS, JOHN, manager of a store in Goochland County, Virginia, 17.. [NAS.B10.12.4.fo.124/127]

SOMERVILLE, ANDREW, born 1781, Kenmore, Perthshire, with wife Janet born 1791, and son John born 1813, emigrated from Port Glasgow to St John, New Brunswick, on the Favorite of St John, master John Hyndman, 22 October 1815. [PANB:MS.RS23E/f9798]

SOMMERVILLE, JOHN, in St Mary's County, Maryland, 1786. [GM#IX.431.112]

SPALDING, JAMES, a merchant in East Florida and in Georgia, 20 October 1772, [NAS.RS27.201.215]

SPEIR, ALEXANDER, Pishenlinn, Moon Township, Pennsylvania, 18 July 1816. [NAS.RD.Renfrew, #6/164]

SPENCE, ALEXANDER, a merchant in Duns, Berwickshire, a bankrupt who escaped to America, around 1795. [NAS.CS230/Sed.Bks.4/3]

SPENCE, ANDREW, died in St Andrew's, Philadelphia, 1805. [AJ#3024]

SPENCE, DAVID, born 1729, a sailor, ran away from the brigantine Chapman, master John Coshare, in the South River, Maryland, on 14 June 1752. [MdGaz#375]

SPENCE, DAVID, in Augusta on 9 November 1827. [NAS.RD5.339.492, 501]

SPENCE, GEORGE, in Albany Fort, North America, son of George Spence a maltman in Dundee, 1745. [NAS.RS35.xvi.117]

SPENCE, GEORGE, and son, settled in St Peter's parish, Prince Edward Island, 1769. [AJ#1332]

SPENCE, JAMES, born 21 December 1756, son of Reverend John Spence and Jean Clow in Orwell, a merchant in Quebec. [F.5.72]

SPENCE, JOHN, from Greenock, in America by 1801. [NAS.CS17.1.9/441]

SPENCE, PETER, a merchant in Virginia, was admitted as a burgess and guildsbrother of Ayr on 7 May 1753. [AyrBR]

SPENCE, ROBERT, a merchant in Kirkcaldy, Fife, released from Edinburgh Tolbooth for transportation to America for 7 years, on 25 July 1769. [NAS.HH11/28]

SPENCE, WALTER, a merchant in New York, son of David Spence a Writer to the Signet, 1789. [NAS.CS17.1.8/42]

SPENCE, WILLIAM, from Maryland, graduated MD from Glasgow University on 30 May 1780; married Isabella, daughter of James Tennant a merchant in Edinburgh, in June 1780. [GM#III/174, 182]

SPENCE, WILLIAM, a tailor from Edinburgh, now in America, 1783. [NAS.CS17.1.2.79]

SPENS, GEORGE, Glasgow, in Philadelphia 1778. [NAS.NRAS.0396.TD37.16]

SPENS, JOCK, Glasgow, in Philadelphia 1778. [NAS.NRAS.0396.TD37.16]

SPENS, ROBERT, a merchant from Glasgow, then in America, 1784. [NAS.CS17.1.3/341]

SPIERS, ALEXANDER, agent in Virginia for Buchanan, Murdoch and Company, in July 1747. [NAS.B10.15.5943]

SPITTAL, JAMES, a vagrant in Portsburgh, Edinburgh, released from Edinburgh Tolbooth for transportation to America via Greenock on 19 July 1773. [NAS.HH11/28]

SPOTSWOOD, ALEXANDER, Major General of Colonel of the American Regiment in Virginia, probate 23 February 1742, Prob.11/716 PCC

SPREULL, ANDREW, of Milton, a merchant in Gosport, Virginia, 1782. [NAS.CS17.1.1.91]

SPROTT, Reverend **JOHN**, born 1780 in Caldons, Stonybank, Wigtown, educated in Stranraer, at Glasgow University, and at Theological Hall from 1805-1807, licensed 1809, joined the relief Church and emigrated to Nova Scotia in 1818, a minister there, died 16 September 1869. [RPC#162]

SPROTT, MARGARET, daughter of Dr George Daniel Sprott, Urbanna, Virginia, 1810. [NAS.CS17.1.31/40]

SQUYRE, JOHN, born 1685, educated at Edinburgh University 1703, a missionary in Carolina 1713-1718, died in Forres, Morayshire, 27 January 1758. [F.6.422]

STARK, DONALD, jr., a tailor in Ollrigg, Caithness, imprisoned as an accessory to housebreaking, theft and robbery, released from Edinburgh Tolbooth for transportation from Leith to Maryland on the Mally of Glasgow, Captain Peacock, 20 September 1769. [NAS.HH11/28]

STARK, HELEN, relict of Archibald Currie, in Richmond, Virginia, grant of Bonnyhill on 20 December 1821. [RGS.165.28.42]

STEDMAN, ROBERT, in Charleston, probate 16 March 1769, Prob.11/953

STEEL, ALEXANDER, from South Uist, emigrated from Tobermory on the Emperor Alexander of Aberdeen, master Alexander Watt, to Sydney, Cape Breton, in July 1823, arrived there on 16 September 1823. [IJ:30.1.1824]

STEEL, JOHN, from South Uist, emigrated from Tobermory on the Emperor Alexander of Aberdeen, master Alexander Watt, to Sydney, Cape Breton, in July 1823, arrived there on 16 September 1823. [IJ:30.1.1824]

STEEL, THOMAS, in Jamaica 1694; returned from Virginia via Newcastle in June 1696, to return to America. [NAS.GD3.5.812, 818]

STEEL, Miss S., from Edinburgh, married M. Drury from Philadelphia, in New York 14 May 1823. [EEC#17471]

STENHOUSE, JOHN, a wright from Greenock, then in America 1796. [NAS.CS17.1.15/399]

STEPHENS, DAVID, son of Mr Stephens a trunkmaker in

Edinburgh, died in New York September 1799.
[AJ#2718]

STEVEN, JAMES, merchant in Virginia, 1789.
[NAS.CS17.1.8/212]

STEVENSON, ANDREW, born 1796, a laborer in Port
Glasgow, emigrated from Port Glasgow to St John,
New Brunswick, on the Favorite of St John, master
John Hyndman, 22 October 1815.
[PANB:MS.RS23E/f9798]

STEVENSON, COLIN, from Coul, Islay, a merchant trading
between Scotland and Newfoundland, 1822.
[NAS.CS17.1.41/673]

STEVENSON, GEORGE, late merchant in Virginia, 1789.
[NAS.CS17.1.8/29]

STEVENSON, HAY, a merchant, died in New York on 19
September 1799. [AJ#2704]

STEVENSON,....., born 1794, a laborer in Port Glasgow,
emigrated from Port Glasgow to St John, New
Brunswick, on the Favorite of St John, master John
Hyndman, 22 October 1815. [PANB:MS.RS23E/f9798]

STEWART, ADAM, late in New York then in Ayr, was
admitted as a burgess and guilds-brother of Ayr on 4
June 1783. [AyrBR]

STEWART, ALEXANDER, son of Reverend James Stewart
{1683-1735} and Elizabeth Campbell, emigrated to
North Carolina. [F.4.169]

STEWART, ALEXANDER, a merchant in Virginia, son of
Samuel Stewart a barber in Greenock, 1789.
[NAS.RS54.2439][NAS.RS81/14]

STEWART, ANGUS, a chapman in Kencroak, Glen Lyon,

Perthshire, now in America, 1795.
[NAS.CS17.1.14/247]

STEWART, ANTHONY, Annapolis, Maryland, 1783.
[NAS.CS17.1.2.149]

STEWART, CHARLES, in Virginia, heir to David Home-
Stewart of Ardgaty, 1788. [NAS.CS17.1.7/333]

STEWART, CHARLES, in Annapolis, Maryland, 1793.
[NAS.CS17.1.12,1793]

STEWART, DANIEL, in Petersburg, Virginia, 1802, 1803.
[NAS.RD3.296.828/RD4.274.501]

STEWART, DAVID, in Annapolis, Maryland, 1793.
[NAS.CS17.1.12]

STEWART, FREDERICK CAMPBELL, of Ascog, late in
Kirnan, Westmoreland County, Virginia, eldest son of
Archibald Stewart of Kirnan, grant of Glassvar on 3
February 1816. [RGS.152.30]

STEWART, HENRY, from Aberdeen, a sailor on the Jupiter
of New York, died in California 1823. [AJ#4036]

STEWART, ISAAC, late Captain of Dunlop's Dragoons in
North America, 1795. [NAS.CS17.1.14/232]

STEWART, JAMES, a merchant in Greenock then in
America, 1790. [NAS.CS17.1.19/319]

STEWART, JAMES, a merchant in New York, 1812.
[NAS.CS230/S13/1]

STEWART, JAMES, from Greenock, a merchant in
Newfoundland, 1813. [NAS.SC53.56.1/iii]

STEWART, JAMES ARROT, son of James Stewart, in New
York, 1820. [NAS.CS17.1.39/140]

STEWART, JOHN, in Virginia, eldest son of the deceased John Stewart factor at Calvin Point, Virginia, for Dunmore Blackburn & Co merchant in Glasgow, 1787. [NAS.CS17.1.6/342]

STEWART, Colonel JOHN, died in Somerset County, Maryland, in June 1794, [EA#3214]

STEWART, NEADRICK, a merchant in Quebec, son of Reverend James Stewart in Anderston, 1824. [NAS.CS17.1.44/46]

STEWART, NEIL, absconded from Portobacco, Maryland, on 3 August 1745. [MdGaz#17]

STEWART, NIEL, late of the Bridge of Tilt now in America, 1782. [NAS.CS17.1.1/290]

STEWART, P., born 1722, late Chief Justice of P.E.I., died on Prince Edward Island 1806. [AJ#3032]

STEWART, ROBERT, born 1791, a laborer in Callendar, emigrated from Port Glasgow to St John, New Brunswick, on the Favorite of St John, master John Hyndman, 22 October 1815. [PANB:MS.RS23E/f9798]

STEWART, ROBERT, sometime in Petersburg, Virginia, then in Nelson County, Virginia, 1818. [NAS.CS17.1.38/313]

STOTHART, ROBERT, from Traquhain, then in Nashville, Tennessee, 1817. [NAS.CS17.1.36/176]

STRANGE, JAMES, in Petersburg, Virginia, 1804. [NAS.NRAS.0607.CBI, bundle 6]

STREHORN, JOHN, late tenant farmer in Clydeneuck, Ayrshire, now in America, 1820. [NAS.CS17.1.39/490]

STRUTHERS, WILLIAM, a merchant in Mobile, 1769.
[NAS.RD4.205.1]

SUTHERLAND, ANN, born 1766, a widow with her family of
four, from Sutherland, emigrated from Cromarty on the
Ossian of Leith, master John Hill, to Pictou in June
1821. [IJ:29.6.1821]

SUTHERLAND, CHARLES, Lieutenant Colonel of the Royal
Newfoundland Fencible Regiment, probate 23 October
1812, Prob.11/1538 PCC

SUTHERLAND, DONALD, born 1775, with his family of six,
from Sutherland, emigrated from Cromarty on the
Ossian of Leith, master John Hill, to Pictou in June
1821. [IJ:29.6.1821]

SUTHERLAND, FRANCIS, a sorner imprisoned in
Edinburgh Tolbooth, released on condition of leaving
Scotland, 5 March 1742. [NAS.HH11/21]

SUTHERLAND, JEAN, born 1799, with his family of one,
from Sutherland, emigrated from Cromarty on the
Ossian of Leith, master John Hill, to Pictou in June
1821. [IJ:29.6.1821]

SUTHERLAND, JOHN, born 1751, with his family of
thirteen, from Sutherland, emigrated from Cromarty on
the Ossian of Leith, master John Hill, to Pictou in June
1821. [IJ:29.6.1821]

SUTTIE, JOHN, now in America 1809.
[NAS.CS17.1.28/276]

SWAN, JAMES, in Boston, 1784. [NAS.CS17.1.3/140]

SWAN, ROBERT, a merchant in Annapolis, Maryland,
(possibly a factor for James Johnston a merchant in
Glasgow), from there to Glasgow on the Mally of
Glasgow, 28 November 1750. [MdGaz#292/293]

SWANSTON, CHARLES, late servant to Mrs Ann Sinclair in Caithness, imprisoned as an accessory to housebreaking, theft and robbery, released from Edinburgh Tolbooth for transportation from Leith to Maryland on the Mally of Glasgow, Captain Peacock, 20 September 1769. [NAS.HH11/28]

SYM, Dr ROBERT, died in Montreal 1807. [AJ#3121]

SYMMER, ALEXANDER, merchant in Maryland, son of Alexander Symmer, a bookseller in Edinburgh, and Elizabeth Forrest (1695-1756). [SM.18.524]

SYMMER, ANDREW, merchant in Maryland, son of Alexander Symmer, a bookseller in Edinburgh, and Elizabeth Forrest (1695-1756). [SM.18.524]

TAIT, JAMES, St Olla, Orkney, on HMS Captain, died in Boston pro. April 1799 PCC

TAIT, WILLIAM, Hudson Bay Company then at the Red River Colony, 1834. [NAS.RS.Orkney.167]

TASKER, DAVID, a merchant in Newfoundland, 1817. [NAS.SC56.53.1/119]

TAYLOR, ALEXANDER, sometime in Montrose, Angus, now in America, 1786. [NAS.CS17.1.5/39]

TAYLOR, COLIN FALCONER, son of the Rector of Musselburgh Grammar School, died in Hamilton, Bermuda, on 3 September 1818. [S#2/97]

TAYLOR, JAMES, son of James Taylor in Norfolk, Virginia, matriculated at Glasgow University on 14 November 1751. [MAGU#45]

TAYLOR, JAMES, jr., late in Fredericton, York County, New Brunswick, then in Port Glasgow, 1818.

[NAS.SC53.56.2/201]

TAYLOR, Mrs MARGARET, wife of John Taylor a merchant
in New York, and daughter of James Scott a merchant
in Glasgow, died 19 November 1797.
[AJ#2609][EWJ#1]

TELFER, Mrs JEAN, relict of Reverend David Somerville
late minister in Strathaven, Lanarkshire, died in
Lexington, Virginia, 1800. [Edinburgh Weekly Journal:
#3.139]

TENANT, JAMES, a clerk in Princess Anne County,
Virginia, probate 20 December 1729, Prob.11/634
PCC

THOM, CHARLES, in Charleston, 27 March 1826.
[NAS.RD5.369.366]

THOMAS, WILLIAM, son of William Thomas a merchant in
Dumfries, a thief imprisoned in Dumfries, transported
from Dumfries to Virginia on the Kirkconnell of
Dumfries in January 1715. [DGA.GF4.19A.10]

THOMPSON, WILLIAM, a servant who absconded from the
Spencer, master Ralph Saddler in the Patuxent River,
Maryland, on 12 March 1748. [MdGaz#153]

THOMSON, ALEXANDER, late HM Customs Collector in
Savannah, Georgia, died in Drummond Street,
Edinburgh, 25 September 1798. [AJ#2648]; Eldest son
of James Thomson and Agnes Smith, a Loyalist from
Savannah, Georgia, died in Edinburgh 1798 aged 64;
his wife Mary Elizabeth Spencer, died in Edinburgh on
2 May 1778 aged 27. [Canongate, Edinburgh,
gravestone]

THOMSON, JAMES. formerly in Leith, a merchant, died in
Washington County, Georgia, 1807. [AJ#3114]

THOMSON, JAMES, late a merchant in Glasgow, died in New York 15 April 1821. [AJ#3826]

THOMSON, WILLIAM, a preacher from Perthshire, married Jean Smith in Ayr 25 January 1775, and immediately went to Virginia. [Ayr Old Parish Register]

THORBURN, WILLIAM, late of the North West Company, died in Cockenzie 3 June 1819. [S#2/126]

TOD, ALEXANDER, a merchant in Philadelphia, 12 August 1777. [NAS.RS27.232/276]

TOD, DAVID, in East Windsor, North America, 1784. [NAS.CS17.1.3/140]

TOD, WILLIAM, a coachmaker in Philadelphia, 12 August 1777. [NAS.RS27.232.276]

TODDIE, LINDSAY, son of Andrew Toddie in St Andrews, died in East Florida 24 February 1820. [S.4.188]

TOMISON, WILLIAM, chief factor at York Fort, Hudson Bay, 1 July 1805. [NAS.RS.Orkney#632; Inv.29.6.1829, Orkney. NAS.CC17.4.1.1.363]

TOVEY, JOHN, in Quebec, 12 October 1830. [NAS.RD5.425.503]

TRAILL, ROBERT, in Portsmouth, New Hampshire, Customs Controller of the Port of Piscataqua, New England, 1768. [NLS#CH3827]

TURNBULL, CHARLES, agent in Virginia for Buchanan, Murdoch and Company, July 1747. [NAS.B10.15.5943]

TURNBULL, JOHN, late of New York, grant of Threaplandhills on 20 December 1803. [RGS.134.108.142]

TURNBULL, JOHN, a merchant from Edinburgh, married Charlotte, youngest daughter of Major Evivitt in Kingston, Upper Canada, 20 July 1821. [EEC#17210]

TURNER, JAMES, a merchant in Virginia, 1782. [NAS.CS17.1.1.97]

TWADDELL, ROBERT, in America, eldest son of Thomas Twaddell a merchant in Dumfries, 1799. [NAS.CS17.1.18/120]

TWATT, MAGNUS, at York Fort, Hudson Bay, 13 December 1806 and 5 June 1807. [NAS.RS.Orkney#695/715]

URQUHART, Reverend, rector of Jamaica parish, Long Island, New York, died 1712. [SPAWI.1712/1168]

VANS, HEW, a merchant in Boston 1750. [NAS.RD2.168.313]

VENNER, JOHN LAUDER, a merchant in St Johns, New Brunswick, grant of Whitslaid on 20 December 1805. [RGS.136.17.26] [NAS.NRAS#0088/B5.28; B5.32/33]

VILANT, DAVID, a merchant in Amboy, New Jersey, formerly a writer in Edinburgh, 1700. [NAS.RD3.91.605]

WADDELL, GEORGE, a merchant from Glasgow, settled in North America by 1806. [NAS.CS17.1.25/329]

WALKER, JOHN, late in Glasgow, now in Boston, 1803. [NAS.AC7.76]

WALKER, MATHEW, from Renfrew, later in America, 1809. [NAS.CS17.1.28/320]

WALKER, ROBERT, in Georgia, 21 November 1825. [NAS.RD5.307.20]

WALKER, WILLIAM, a merchant in Virginia, then in Glasgow, testament confirmed on 29 December 1786 in Glasgow. [NAS]

WALLACE, HUGH, a weaver from Glasgow, settled in Dalhousie township, Upper Canada, around 1821. [BPP.2.167]

WALLACE, MICHAEL, merchant and factor in Virginia, husband of Margaret Cross, resident partner of John Wallace and Company in Virginia, 1771-1775. [NAS.B10.13.4.fo.8]

WALLACE, ..., a merchant from Leith, now in America, 1800. [NAS.CS17.1.18/416]

WARDEN, JAMES, a merchant in Boston 1774, son of the late James Warden a shipmaster in Greenock and grandson of the deceased Robert Warden. [NAS.RS81/9]

WARDROP, DANIEL, a merchant 1765-1791, died in Virginia. [NAS.B10.13.4.fo.8]

WARDROP, JOHN, a merchant in Maryland, probate 1 July 1767, Prob.11/931 PCC

WARDROP, JOHN, from Glasgow, died in Brunswick County, Virginia, on 31 March 1789. [GM##XII.594.174]

WARK, JOHN, late in Hazletown now in America 1805. [NAS.CS17.1.24/271]

WATSON, JAMES, born 1793, arrived in St John, New Brunswick, in November 1815 on the Favorite of St John, master John Hindman, from Scotland.

[PANB:MS.RS555/c4]

WATSON, JEREMIAH, a baker in America, 1795.
[NAS.CS17.1.14,340]

WATSON, JOHN, son of Reverend Watson in Glasgow,
died Point St Charles, near Montreal, 6 May 1820.
[S.4.183][EA#5910]

WATSON, SAMUEL, with four others, emigrated from
Campbelltown to Cape Fear, North Carolina, on the
Edinburgh of Campbelltown, 27 July 1771.
[NAS.SC54.2.106]

WATSON, WILLIAM, possibly from Old Kilpatrick,
Dunbartonshire, a stonemason in Pittsburgh,
Pennsylvania, 1801. [NLS.Acc.7439]

WATT, ANDREW, son of the late Andrew Watt a mason in
Perth, a merchant who settled in America by 1806.
[NAS.CS17.1.25/493]

WATT, STEPHEN, a coal-driver in Stobsmain, imprisoned in
Dalkeith, later in Edinburgh Tolbooth, released to go
abroad as banished from Scotland for life, on 25
September 1744. [NAS.HH11/22]

WEIR, ALEXANDER, late in America, now in Edinburgh,
1790. [NAS.CS17.1.9, 329]

WEIR, GEORGE, a merchant in Virginia then in London,
1801, son of James Weir a shipmaster in Port
Glasgow. [NAS.RS81.21.77, fo.77]

WEIR, JAMES, a merchant in Virginia, 1787.
[NAS.CS17.1.6/268]

WELCH, MARGARET, second daughter of William Welch a
merchant in New York, married Edward MacKenzie, a
merchant in Glasgow, 27 October 1823. [DPCA#1110]

WELCH, Captain SAMUEL, New York, was admitted as a burgess and guilds-brother of Ayr on 9 February 1708. [AyrBR]

WHIBSTER, JOHN, Hudson Bay Company, 1794. [NAS.RS.Caithness#266]

WHITE, ANDREW, a merchant in Norfolk, Virginia {?}, then in Greenock, testament confirmed 3 January 1766 and 7 October 1776 in Glasgow. [NAS]

WHITE, ARCHIBALD, sometime merchant in Norfolk, Virginia, then in Greenock, deceased by 1763, son of Daniel White a tobacconist in Greenock.[NAS.RS81.7.496]

WHITE, ROBERT, sometime tenant in Cockenzie, now in North America, 1821. [NAS.CS17.1.40/223]

WHITTET, ROBERT, in Pennsylvania 1823. [NAS.SC48.49.25.19.61]

WILKINSON, DOLLIE, a vagrant and thief, transported as an indentured servant by James Corbet, a merchant in Dumfries, to America in 1737. [DGA.Misc.RB2.2.169]

WILLIAMS, DAVID, born 1792, arrived in St John, New Brunswick, in November 1815, on the Favorite of St John, master John Hindman, from Scotland. [PANB:MS.RS555/c4]

WILLIAMSON, DAVID, born in Fife 1764, for 30 years pastor of an Associate Congregation in Whitehaven, New England, died in New York 18 May 1822. [AJ#3839][S.5.237]

WILLIAMSON, GEORGE, a merchant in Richmond, Virginia, 1823. [NAS.CS17.1.42/613]

WILLIAMSON, JAMES, a tailor from Glasgow in Virginia, 1783, 1790. [NAS.CS17.1.2.254; CS17.1.9,116]

WILLIAMSON, JOHN, a merchant from Glasgow who settled in America by 1803. [NAS.CS17.1.22/247]

WILLIAMSON, WALTER, son of Walter Williamson deceased, surgeon in Virginia, 1786. [NAS.CS17.1.5/27]

WILSON, ALLAN, a mason in Florida, 1819. [NAS.CS17.1.39/633]

WILSON, ALLAN, a farmer in Florida 1814. [NAS.CS17.11.34/94]

WILSON, ARCHIBALD, late of Honey Farm, Orange County, Virginia, now in Greenock, 1806. [GA.T-ARD#13/1]

WILSON, DAVID, late a ships carpenter in Greenock, now in America, 1789. [NAS.CS17.1.8/317]

WILSON, Dr GEORGE, of Stottencleugh, late a physician in Petersburg, Virginia, died in London 13 October 1799. [AJ#2703][SM.61.907]

WILSON, JACOBINA, merchant in Ayr, and her husband N. Northfleet late of Virginia, 1797. [NAS.CS17.1.16/190]

WILSON, JAMES, born in Glasgow, formerly a resident of New England but then a widower in Rotterdam, the Netherlands, married Margaret Durham, from Kirkcaldy, Fife, in Rotterdam on 25 March 1691. [Records of the Scots Kirk in Rotterdam: I.356]

WILSON, JAMES F., born 1789, son of Alexander Wilson a merchant in Inverness, settled in New Orleans, died in Virginia 5 October 1821. [AJ#3866][EEC#17257]

WILSON, JOHN, a farmer from Kirkland, Dreghorn, Ayrshire, later in America by 1812. [NAS.CS17.1.31/422]

WILSON, THOMAS, a mason from Fife, settled in Prince Edward Island by 1818. [NLS.Acc.6981]

WILSON, WILLIAM, a merchant in Boston, New England, was admitted as a burgess and guildsbrother of Ayr on 29 March 1716. [AyrBR]

WILSON, WILLIAM, in New York, 1820, [NAS.CS17.1.39/579]; 18 December 1829. [NAS.RD5.418.689]

WILSON, WILLIAM, jr., a merchant in Glasgow now in Virginia, 1786. [NAS.CS17.1.5/351]

WINDRICK, JANET, late servant to Magnus Chambers a farmer at Grimness, South Ronaldsay, Orkney Islands, a prisoner in Inverness Tolbooth, guilty of child-murder, was banished to the American Plantations on 29 May 1769, imprisoned in Leith Tolbooth, released for shipment from Leith to Maryland on the Mally of Glasgow, Captain Peacock, on 20 September 1769. [NAS.HH11/28]

WISHART, ALEXANDER, a Lieutenant of the 42nd Regiment, on half-pay, died in York, Upper Canada, 10 December 1823.[Fife Herald #113][East Preston Street cemetery, Edinburgh]

WOOD, JOHN, merchant in Flower de Hundred, Virginia, 1783. [NAS.CS17.1.2.170]

WOOD, JOHN, born in Scotland, died in Richmond, Virginia, 15 May 1822. [EEC#17327]

WOOD, JOHN, from Netherwood, Dumfriesshire, died in Richmond, Virginia, 25 December 1822. [EEC#17415]

WOODS, JAMES, a merchant in America, then in Ayr, 1787. [NAS.CS17.1.6/334]

WOTHERSPOON, JAMES, eldest son of James Wotherspoon in Rutherglen, Lanarkshire, emigrated from Old Monklands, near Glasgow to America around 1733, resident with John Parnham a merchant in Charles County, Maryland, a merchant on the James River, Virginia, from 1733 to 1738, sought in 1748. [MdGaz#198][VaGaz#112][NAS.B64.1.6.5.7]

WRIGHT, ARCHIBALD CURRIE, a bank note forger, petitioned for and was granted banishment to the American Plantations, in Edinburgh 10 August 1747. [CM#4187]

WRIGHT, GEORGE, late in New York now in Glasgow, 1782. [NAS.CS17.1.1.351]

WRIGHT, JAMES, in Bridge of Weir, to emigrate via Quebec to Upper Canada, 1820. [NAS.SC58.75.79]

WYLLIE, HUGH, in Virginia, 1794. [NAS.CS17.1.13,152]

WYNN, EDWARD, a sailor in North America, father of Peter Robertson Wynn, a soldier of the 78th Regiment, 15 July 1839. [NAS.S/H]

YORSTON, ROBERT, at York Factory, Hudson Bay, son of Robert Yorston, a farmer in Harray, Orkney, 29 January 1810. [NAS.RS.Orkney #789]

YOUNG, ANDREW, a farmer from Westmuir, then in North America by 1797. [NAS.CS17.1.16/257]

YOUNG, ANDREW, a biscuit baker in Richmond, Virginia, 1815, brother of William Young in Trelawney, Jamaica, sons of ..... Young in Uphall, West Lothian. [NAS.RH1.2.804]

YOUNG, JOHN, Colonel of HM Royal American Regiment, husband of Ann Pringle, 1761. [NAS.RS27.157.341]

YOUNG, JOHN, in Greensborough, USA, 1824. [NAS.CS17.1.44/50]

YUILL, JAMES, Truro, Halifax, Nova Scotia, probate 10 August 1812, Prob.11/1536 PCC

YUILL, JOHN, from Glasgow, then in Boston or Jamaica, son of Alexander Yuill a merchant in Boston, 1782. [NAS.CS17.1.1.307]

YUILLE, THOMAS, a merchant in Virginia, deceased, 7 May 1748. [NAS.B10.12.1.fo.178]

www.ingramcontent.com/pod-product-compliance
Lightning Source LLC
Chambersburg PA
CBHW050525270326
41926CB00015B/3069